CW01083095

75

Years *of*
INDIAN ECONOMY

Also by the author

Beyond Covid's Shadow: Mapping India's Economic Resurgence (ed.)

The Bombay Plan: Blueprint for Economic Resurgence
(co-authored with Meghnad Desai)

JOURNEY *of a* NATION

Years *of*
INDIAN ECONOMY

Re-emerge, Reinvest, Re-engage

SANJAYA BARU

RUPA

Published by
Rupa Publications India Pvt. Ltd 2022
7/16, Ansari Road, Daryaganj
New Delhi 110002

Sales centres:
Allahabad Bengaluru Chennai
Hyderabad Jaipur Kathmandu
Kolkata Mumbai

ISBN: 978-93-5520-361-8

Third impression 2022

10 9 8 7 6 5 4 3

Contents

Introduction

This book has been written for the post-millennial generation. A millennial, according to several dictionaries, is a person reaching adulthood in the early twenty-first century. This book is for the post-millennial generation that is reaching young adulthood as India celebrates 75 years of Independence. I have tried to keep it deliberately simple—devoid of the jargon that makes economists imagine that their discipline is more a science than an art that ought to be housed in a school of 'social sciences' rather than that of the humanities. Fortunately, for those of us who have chosen to be students of 'political economy' rather than view economics as a science, bolstered by 'econometrics', the growing appeal of behavioural economics, and the fact that many Nobel Prizes in Economics have been awarded to behavioural economists, has helped focus attention on human, especially political, agency in economic policymaking.

It is an interesting fact that the discipline of political economy and economics captured the attention of bright young Indians in the very early years of the national movement. As I repeatedly remind my readers further in this book, by the 1890s, Indian national leaders were already drawing lessons from the economic rise of Japan, Asia's first industrial nation. The engineer Sir Mokshagundam Visvesvaraya, who founded the Institution of Engineers (India) (IEI) and built great projects like the Krishna Raja Sagara Dam, returned from a visit to Japan and gave a clarion call to fellow Indians in 1898, 'Industrialize or perish!'

Three years later, in 1901, Dadabhai Naoroji estimated the 'drain of wealth' as a consequence of British rule and attributed colonial India's backwardness to this fact in his book *Poverty and Un-British Rule in India*. Quite understandably, as we note in the first two chapters, a growing awareness of the economic history and political economy of colonial rule began to shape the national movement for freedom. A generation of bright young Indians and Europeans studied the ill effects of colonialism and feudalism on the social and economic welfare of Indians. This awareness fuelled Indian nationalism at the beginning of the twentieth century with Naoroji, Gopal Krishna Gokhale, Mahadev Govind Ranade, Bal Gangadhar Tilak and others launching the swadeshi movement. Mahatma Gandhi further empowered the concept by defining swadeshi as being at the heart of his call for swaraj (self-rule).

These 'homespun' ideas were also greatly influenced by the development and industrialization experience of the Soviet Union, which, by the 1940s, had emerged as a great industrial and military power. Thus, two grand ideas began to shape Indian political thinking on economic policy by the middle of the twentieth century—one, the ideas espoused by Gandhiji and Gandhians, who believed in the preservation and promotion of *gram swaraj* or cottage and village industry, and small-scale industry; second, the views of Indian business and political leadership who pushed for large-scale and modern industrialization, mimicking the Soviet model. We shall look at each of these ideas and how they shaped policy.

The structure of this book is not purely chronological, nor have I tried to cover each and every aspect of the economy and economic policy. I have tried to focus on key ideas and events that have shaped policy and its impact, with a conscious attempt not to bombard my reader with too many numbers. If data is ever mentioned, it is only because such facts are relevant to the story of India's economic resurgence. The title of this book refers to India re-emerging as an economy. Western economic and business analysts have usually referred to India and other newly industrializing economies as 'emerging economies'. Surely, most of them are 'emerging' from long years of underdevelopment and exploitation under colonial rule. But the term 'emerging' hides the fact that some developing economies, especially China and India, are, in fact, 're-emerging' rather than merely emerging. They have re-emerged into the foray as strong contenders for the leading global economies from the setbacks caused by two to three centuries of European colonial rule.

Through his accurate historical and statistical work, the British historian Angus Maddison in *The World Economy: A Millennial Perspective,* estimated that in 1700, China and India together accounted for half of the world's national income and that by 1950, their combined share was down to less than 10 per cent. Despite having endured successive waves of foreign invaders, the fact is that by 1700, the Indian subcontinent stretched from Afghanistan to present-day Myanmar and from the Himalayas to the Indian Ocean, and was home to vibrant agrarian and trading economies. India's economic footprint spanned across the Eurasian landmass and the Indian Ocean, reaching as far as the Mediterranean in the west and Vietnam in the east. The Mughal Empire and various other kingdoms outside it were reasonably prosperous and linked to the global economy.

European colonialism disrupted these links and impoverished the economy, imposing an economic system that shrunk these economies. In response to the pain and poverty this imposed on the people of the subcontinent, a national movement emerged, demanding 'swaraj' and 'freedom'. In 1947, India declared itself a sovereign democratic republic and adopted a constitution that created 'India, that is Bharat' as a 'Union of States'. The first government of independent India soon settled down to the business of promoting national economic development. This book offers a glimpse of that history and presents a brief assessment of the state of the economy today, 75 years after Independence.

The 1950s were momentous and were defined by the ascendance of ideas that favoured industrialization. On the other hand, the 1960s was a decade of crisis in which the economy became more insular, and government regulation and control became more pervasive and detrimental to the growth of Indian enterprise. A gradual change in thinking was evident in the following decade, but its true impact was felt only in the 1980s. The Green Revolution in agriculture took root in the 1970s and created a politically influential rural rich in the 1980s. Over the 30 years from 1950 to 1980, India's gross domestic product (GDP) or national income, grew at an annual average of 3.5 per cent; and in the following two decades, 1980–2000, it grew at 5.5 per cent.

Through these decades, the regional pattern of development first noticed in the first half of the twentieth century became reinforced by the regionally differentiated impact of the Green Revolution. Thus, western and large parts of northwestern and peninsular India, including states like Andhra Pradesh, Gujarat, Haryana, Karnataka, Maharashtra, Punjab and Tamil Nadu, became the more developed states. While West Bengal was also classified as a developed state, it became far too dependent on traditional sectors like coal, jute, iron and steel, while new industries like automobiles and pharmaceuticals were located away in western and southern India. For a long time, the laggard states—Bihar, Madhya Pradesh, Rajasthan and Uttar Pradesh—were referred to as BIMARU ('bimar' means sick or ill in Hindi).

The year 1991 was the turning point for the economy. I have devoted an entire chapter to it, drawing from my book titled *1991: How P.V. Narasimha Rao Made History*. Many have often argued that if India secured political independence in 1947, it acquired economic liberation in 1991. There is no doubt that after 1947, the year 1991 was a landmark year for the country and the economy. Not only did India come out of the worst economic crisis since the 1960s, but more importantly, 1991 marked a break from the regime of what some have called 'bureaucratic socialism', with its array of regulations and controls. The policies introduced in 1991 have been continued and brought forward by successive governments of different political hues. Even though the Bharatiya Janata Party (BJP) opposed the reform initiatives of 1991, it chose not vote against the government on the floor of Parliament during its first two years in office, and efforts made after that bore no fruit. The Narasimha Rao government lasted its full term till 1996. The government of Atal Bihari Vajpayee took the reform initiatives forward through its six years in office from 1998 to 2004.

While the rate of economic growth began picking up in the 1980s, it imposed several costs, including unsustainable external debt and a rising fiscal deficit in government finances. These contributed, among other factors, to the balance of payments crisis of 1991. Once remedial action was taken, with the fiscal deficit reduced, and trade and industrial policy liberalized, the rate of investment began picking up. During the period 2000–2015, the economy grew at an annual average of 7.5 per cent, with the so-called 'golden years of growth', 2003–2008, recording close to 9 per cent growth.

The first two decades of the twenty-first century have witnessed a significant transformation of the economy. There was a perceptible reduction in poverty, a rapid spread of urbanization and the establishment of a globally competent services economy. India led the world in the production of several agricultural commodities. However, the manufacturing sector remained a laggard, despite the launch of a new 'manufacturing strategy' by the Manmohan Singh government in 2012 that was subsequently modified and relaunched as the Make in India and Atmanirbhar Bharat programmes by the Narendra Modi government.

The demonetization of high-value currency notes in November 2016 destabilized the economy, and after 2018, new concerns have emerged on the economic front, including a decline in the rate of investment, continued stagnation in the share of manufacturing in national income, and the loss of momentum in export growth. To add to these concerns, the nationwide lockdown imposed in response to the Covid-19 pandemic and the uncertainty generated both by contingency measures and the pandemic itself has cast a long shadow on economic growth.

India entered the 75th year of Independence, still carrying grave concerns about poverty, unemployment, inflation and loss of global competitiveness. Despite these setbacks, in terms of purchasing power parity, India is the world's third-largest economy behind the United States (US) and China. In US dollar terms, it is now the world's sixth-largest economy, behind the US, China, Japan, Germany and the United Kingdom (UK). I have deliberately left out of this book any discussion of recent policy changes as well as of recent developments such as the emergence of start-ups, the rapid growth of a digital economy and the plans to localize defence manufacturing and reduce dependence on imports. These developments need to be sustained for one to assess their impact.

This brief book, written for a non-specialist audience, tells the story of India's economic rise over the past 75 years. I have tried to tell it in as simple a language as possible for any young person to read and understand. I offer here what are essentially my views based on my reading of important books and articles on the economy. I have not tried to present before the reader all the different views that are part of the ongoing debates on the economy but have cited a few books and essays that an interested reader may wish to peruse.

US President Harry Truman once demanded, 'Give me a one-handed economist!' Frustrated, he explained, 'All my economists say, "on the one hand...on the other..."' Keeping in mind the cautious position taken by many economists, and the fear and intimidation of the jargon that presents itself as a hurdle to the interests of the laypersons who may be curious about this field, in the following pages, I have attempted a much less indecisive peek into Indian economy. Those interested in entering this vast edifice of knowledge may do so using the key of a professional course in economics. However, you do not need anything more than adequate knowledge of the English language to follow this simple introduction to the 're-emergence' of the Indian economy as a vibrant engine of growth and development.

From Dominance to 'The Drain'

Owing to the painstaking statistical compilation and analysis undertaken by historian Angus Maddison, there is now global recognition of the fact that for over a millennium preceding the European colonization of Asia, India and China were the world's biggest economies.[1] Taken together, the national income or the GDP of the two economies accounted for more than half the world GDP during most of the first millennium of the Christian era (CE) (Figure 1.1). Even in terms of per capita national income, China and India were ahead of Europe and much of the world. Maddison estimated that India's per capita income in 1000 CE was 450 international dollars. This compared with China's 466 and Western Europe's 427.[2] The dominance of Asia in the world economy was evident in the world average per capita income during the same period, which was 453. It took 700 years for Western Europe to catch up with China and India and another century for its share of world income to exceed China's. A gradual decline in India's share occurred over the second millennium, but the sharpest fall began in the early 1700s and continued unabated till the middle of the twentieth century.

For a variety of reasons, ranging from the application of modern science and technology, social and cultural practices, political institutions and so on, the period AD 1000 to AD 1700 saw Western Europe increasing its share of world income and China succeeding in maintaining it, while India experienced only a gradual decline in its share. The advent of European colonialism and conquest hastened this decline for India. Yet, throughout this entire period—from the pre-Christian era till the middle of the second millennium—the Indian subcontinent was home to a vibrant economy endowed with an abundance of natural resources, human skills and the entrepreneurial spirit of its trading communities.

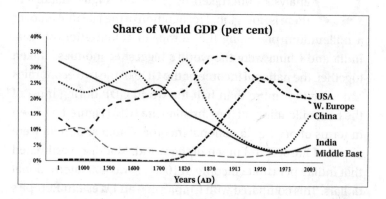

Figure 1.1: Share of World National Income (Gross Domestic Product)

Source: Data from Maddison, Angus, *Contours of the World Economy 1–2030 AD: Essays in Macro-Economic History*, Oxford University Press, Oxford, 2007.

India, as we know it today, was neither a sovereign nation nor an integrated economy till it attained independence from colonial rule. Pre-Independence India had pockets of active enterprise, productive agriculture and urbanization. It also had large tracts of economic backwardness. The regions that were economically more developed abutted major rivers and spread across their deltas. Urban settlements, too, came up along rivers that were then linked to the seas beyond. The best proof of the quality and level of economic activity across the subcontinent is its trade with the rest of the world. Indian trading communities were linked both by land and sea to regions across Asia and the Indian Ocean littoral. Merchant communities in western, northwestern and southern regions were actively engaged in trade, both across the seas and across the Eurasian and Southeast Asian regions. The modern states of Gujarat, Kerala and Andhra Pradesh were home to ancient ports that linked the subcontinent's economy to Arabia, Persia and beyond, all the way to Europe in the west, and as far as Vietnam in Southeast Asia. India was at the crossroads of both sea- and land-based trade with regions around it.

In his rare classic *India and the Indian Ocean: An Essay on the Influence of Sea Power on Indian History*, the historian K.M. Pannikar reminded us, 'Millenniums before Columbus sailed the Atlantic and Magellan crossed the Pacific, the Indian Ocean had become an active thoroughfare of commercial and cultural traffic.'[3] Thanks in part to its geography, given the annual and seasonal flow of winds, the sociology of the enterprising traders of Gujarat and the Coromandel Coast, and the Arab traders, the Indian Ocean was one of the early theatres of maritime trade and cultural intercourse, and India was at the centre of its maritime trading activity. The Srivijaya Empire, based in Sumatra, dominated the eastern seaboard of the Indian Ocean well into the tenth century. 'The period of Hindu supremacy in the Ocean was one of complete freedom of trade and navigation,' records Pannikar.[4] With the decline of Hindu kingdoms in India and Southeast Asia, Arab rulers and merchants gained dominance over the Indian Ocean.

In his masterly study of civilization and capitalism from the fifteenth to the eighteenth centuries, the historian Fernand Braudel draws attention to the dominant presence of India in the Indian Ocean region.[5] Braudel refers to the region spanning the Arabian Sea, the Bay of Bengal, the Straits of Malacca and the South China Sea—what is now referred to as the Indo-Pacific—as the 'greatest of all the world economies' of the pre-industrial, pre-capitalist era. According to Braudel:

> The Far East, taken as a whole, consisted of three gigantic world-economies: Islam, overlooking the Indian Ocean from the Red Sea and the Persian Gulf, and controlling the endless chain of deserts stretching across Asia from Arabia to China; India, whose influence extended throughout the Indian Ocean, both east and west of Cape Comorin; and China, at once a great territorial power—striking deep into the heart of Asia—and a maritime force, controlling the seas and countries bordering the Pacific. And so it had been for many hundreds of years.[6]

Braudel goes on to say:

> The relationship between these huge areas, was the result of a series of pendulum movements of greater or lesser strength, either side of the centrally positioned Indian subcontinent. The swing might benefit first the East and then the West, redistributing functions, power and political or economic advance. Through all these

vicissitudes, however, India maintained her central position: her merchants in Gujarat and on the Malabar and Coromandel coasts prevailed for centuries against their many competitors—the Arab traders of the Red Sea, the Persian merchants of the Gulf, or the Chinese merchants familiar with the Indonesian seas to which their junks were now regular visitors.

As Nayan Chanda records in his study of precolonial globalization, Arab and Indian traders together worked the supply chains that linked the Indian economy to global markets.[7]

If the waters around the Indian peninsula were one route for trade with the world, the deserts, forests and mountains on top, from northwest to northeast, were no barriers either. There was considerable movement of traders across the Eurasian landmass through Central Asia, Tibet and Southeast Asia. A large part of India's trade with the Eurasian landmass— right up to Europe—was by land and passed through what are now Pakistan and Afghanistan. The historian Scott C. Levi has recorded the role played by 'Hindu traders', the Khatri community of what are now Pakistan and Indian Punjab. For centuries they financed and facilitated trade between India and Central Asia and regions beyond, all the way to Europe.[8] The prominent historian Sanjay Subrahmanyam's exhaustive work on trade in precolonial India shows the extent and range of commercial interaction India had with the world around it. To quote: 'Whereas during the years 800–1300, the main axis of long-distance commercial flows in Asia appears to have been in the east-west direction (both in the caravan routes through Central Asia and on sea), the years after 1300 saw

the rise of commerce largely in the north-south direction.'[9]
Gujarat, Andhra Pradesh and the Tamil regions boasted of
the most active trading communities.

The prosperity of the southern kingdoms was based both
on their thriving domestic economies and their trading links
with Southeast Asia. The kingdoms of Vijayanagara, Kakatiya,
Chera, Chola, Pandava and the subsequent kingdoms of the
region like Hyderabad, Mysuru and Travancore were marked
by agrarian prosperity, visionary leadership and active trading
communities. Many of them promoted art and culture and
the spread of education.

While the subcontinent's enduring and extensive overseas
trade points to the vibrancy of the precolonial economy,
medieval India was also characterized by extreme inequality
with a relatively small elite enjoying opulent lifestyles and
an impoverished, and therefore, not very productive, mass
of peasants and labourers. Maddison attributes the steady
decline in India's share of world GDP through the Mughal
period to the low productivity of land and labour, low
subsistence incomes of the indigent masses and the usurious
rates of taxation that filled the coffers of the ruling elites. The
extravagant lifestyle of India's ruling class is known to have
surpassed that of the European aristocracy of the time. To
quote Maddison, 'The Mughals had the military power to
squeeze a large surplus from a passive village society. The
ruling class had an extravagant lifestyle whose needs were
supplied by urban artisans producing high-quality cotton
textiles, silks, jewellery, decorative swords and weapons.'[10]

Challenging the view that the precolonial Indian
economy was prosperous, Maddison has suggested that the
highly exploitative character of the tax regime in Mughal India

and its feudal social structure impeded social development and economic progress. India had more urban centres than Europe, and Indian artisans produced goods that found a global market. Indian textiles were in great demand globally. There was little that India needed from the rest of the world, so it earned gold and silver in exchange for all the goods it exported. The problem, however, was that all this wealth was concentrated in a few hands and few places. While the West made good use of its growing knowledge of science and technology in the centuries following the Renaissance; at the same time, in precolonial India, the level of social development lagged behind.

What was true for the Mughal Empire was also true for the many Hindu kingdoms. The economic inequality they engendered was made worse by the social inequality of the caste system. It was into this society—divided between the rich and the poor, prosperity and impoverishment, growth and stagnation—that the Europeans first arrived. For centuries the relationship between Europe and India was through mutually beneficially trade. However, once Europe acquired mastery over maritime and military technology, built large ships and equipped them with offensive and defensive firepower, it was able to dominate this trade by controlling the seas through which such trade was conducted.

Asserting dominance in the waters around India in the seventeenth and early eighteenth centuries, European powers took control of the existing and thriving maritime trade. Using firepower mounted on ships, European gunboats pushed Indian and Chinese maritime traders out of the waters, around the peninsula and established their oligopolistic control over India's maritime trade. Having done so, they changed the nature of India's trading relationship with the world by making India a source of raw materials, natural resources and labour, and a market for European finished goods. This, in turn, had a debilitating impact on the subcontinent's economy. External trade was no longer an opportunity; it became an imposition. The institution that facilitated this was the English East India Company (EIC).

Arriving on Indian shores as traders, the EIC created an armed force, initially to protect its trading interests, that defeated the army of the nawab of Oudh, Siraj ud-Daulah, at Plassey in Bengal in 1757 and took formal control of the administration of the region. Soon, the English established their presence along the Coromandel Coast, administering the region from Fort St George, now in Chennai. By the end of the eighteenth century, Britain emerged as the dominant European colonizer across the subcontinent. Of all the European mercantile interests that arrived at Indian ports, it was the English EIC that emerged as the dominant player. Having arrived as traders, the English soon became rulers, establishing an empire that was financed by the toil of the subject people. Taking control of large parts of the Mughal Empire, the EIC funded its administration and trade with India, exporting commodities, goods and raw materials, out of tax revenues it collected from Indians.

In his highly readable account of the history of the EIC, historian William Dalrymple reminds us that one of the first Indian language words to enter the English language was 'loot'.[11] It is this loot of Indian wealth and income that the nationalist business leader Dadabhai Naoroji famously described as 'the drain'.[12] The subjugation of the Mughal economy to the needs of British business and the consequent enrichment of the British economy was undertaken with Indian funds, raised as taxes from Indian producers, and collected by an administration and an army manned by Indians. The steep decline in India's share of world income, as shown by Maddison, was the consequence of this drain and the parasitical nature of European colonialism.

National Movement and Economic Thinking

I n a seminal essay quantifying the exact 'drain' of Indian wealth and income as a consequence of British imperial administration, economists Utsa and Prabhat Patnaik have estimated it—cumulated up to the year 2020—to be '£13.39 *trillion*, over four times the United Kingdom's estimated GDP for that year.'[1] As Dadabhai Naoroji first explained and the Patnaiks later established in great detail, the so-called 'drain of wealth' from India was engineered by ensuring that a third of the rupee tax revenues collected in India by the EIC was, in fact, not spent in India but was used to finance the acquisition and export of goods to Britain and the rest of the world.

This drain had internal and external components. The revenue paid by producers and cultivators to the foreign entity was never ploughed back as investment by the State or as expenditure on public service, except in some pockets. This was the internal drain that went to fund the foreign entity. The Indians who paid these taxes were peasants, artisans and small business owners since there was hardly any Indian-owned big business till the 1930s. The tax so collected would be used to pay these economic agents for whatever product or material was bought from them to be exported by the British trading firm. This means the Indian producer's income taken away as tax would return to her as payment for goods sold by the trading firm at multiple times the cost price. These profits accrued to the trading firm and not the producer.

This share of national income that was collected as tax revenue was then used as 'expenditure abroad', as the Patnaiks explain:

> [A]s reimbursement to the producers for their export surplus with the world [...] This export surplus earned specie and sterling, which was entirely siphoned off for its own use by the colonizing power via manipulated accounting mechanisms. [...] This direct linking of the fiscal system with the trade system is the essence of drain in colonies where the producers were not slaves but nominally free petty producers, namely tax-paying peasants and artisans.[2]

The EIC and its successor regime, the British imperial government in India, created new systems of revenue administration that had varying impacts on the agrarian economy of the subcontinent. In Greater Bengal, or what was later known as West Bengal, Bihar and Odisha, and the United and Central Provinces (Uttar Pradesh and Madhya Pradesh), the revenue system was called the 'permanent settlement' and depended on a class of zamindars who were tasked to collect revenue from the direct producers and hand a fixed amount—89 per cent—to the State and retain only 11 per cent. The institutionalization of an intermediary between the direct producer and the State, namely the rent-collecting landlord, and the high rate of taxation imposed, was not only oppressive to the direct producers but also offered little incentive to either the zamindar or the British to invest in land improvement. Hence, over time, the agrarian economy in these regions declined as the productivity of land and labour did not improve to keep pace with the rising population.

An alternative system of revenue collection, called the ryotwari system, under which farmers paid rent directly to the administration, was regarded as more progressive since it offered the administration an incentive to invest in productivity-enhancing policies and schemes, given that as farmers' incomes improved, the revenue of the administration went up. Provinces in western and northwestern India, covering Bombay and Punjab, as well as Madras, had the ryotwari system in place. These regions accounted for much of the improvement in agricultural production, productivity and farmers' incomes during this period.

Largely, due to this varying regional pattern of revenue systems, the regional pattern of agricultural development was also varied. As the American economist George Blyn showed in his pioneering study of regional agricultural trends between 1891 and 1941, growth in foodgrain production exceeded population growth in the Bombay, Punjab and Madras regions, while it lagged behind it in the Bengal and the Uttar Pradesh and Central Province regions.[3]

The rapacious alienation of income and wealth by the EIC and its successor government of British India left the Indian economy impoverished, contributing to rising nationalist consciousness against colonial dominance and the subsequent anti-colonial mobilization. The poor state of the economy was reflected in the condition of human and social development, with high rates of infant mortality, poverty and ill-health, and low literacy rates.

Several developments around the beginning of the twentieth century shaped Indian thinking about the importance of industrialization and modernization, and the negative economic impact of foreign rule. The communist revolution in Russia in 1917, the weakening of European power as a consequence of the First World War and the rise of Asian nationalism, first in Japan, then in India, and subsequently across Asia, contributed to a change in British imperial policy in India. During the interwar period, the government of British India began to make policy decisions aimed at promoting economic development. We have already drawn attention to the realization that British colonialism had drained a large share out of India's national wealth and produce. Running parallel to this growing awareness about the exploitative nature of colonialism was the rising consciousness of another Asian nation that had kept Europeans at bay, had done well for itself and was industrializing as a sovereign nation. This was the small island nation of Japan.

Among the prominent Indians who had visited Japan and were impressed by its scientific and technological prowess combined with deep patriotism and a distinctly Japanese way of life was Swami Vivekananda. On his sea voyage to Chicago in 1893, where he addressed the World Congress of Religions, Swami Vivekananda met industrialist Jamsetji Tata. The two had stopped over in Japan and had long conversations about Japan's modernization and its lessons for India. On his return to India, Tata sought and secured Swamiji's blessings for setting up the Indian Institute of Science. The engineer

Sir M. Visvesvaraya, the founder of the IEI and the Mysore Chamber of Commerce, returned home from a visit to Japan in 1898, hugely impressed by its economic development and industrial prowess and gave India the slogan, 'Industrialize or perish!' Viswesvarayya was the first engineer to be honoured with a Bharat Ratna in 1955, the second being Dr A.P.J. Abdul Kalam four decades later.

In 1916, Rabindranath Tagore travelled to Japan. He visited the country a decade after Japan's famous victory over Russia in 1905. That was a landmark event in the history of the world because Japan was the first Asian nation to defeat a European country. Japan's victory inspired India's national leadership, and Tagore wrote lyrically about Japan's rise:

> [M]odern Japan has come out of the immemorial East like a lotus blossoming in easy grace, all the while keeping its firm hold upon the profound depth from which it has sprung. [...] She has shown her bold spirit in breaking through the confinements of habits, useless accumulations of the lazy mind, seeking safety in its thrift and its locks and keys. Thus she has come in contact with the living time and has accepted with eagerness and aptitude the responsibilities of modern civilization. This it is which has given heart to the rest of Asia.[4]

There was considerable awareness among educated Indians, specially trained economists, of the extent of and limits to development in India. The economist Jayasankar Krishnamurty of the Delhi School of Economics in his edited volume, *Towards Development Economics: Indian Contributions 1900-1945*, has put together some of the more important essays written by Indian economists through the first half of the twentieth century, analysing the state of the economy and pointing to the kind of policy intervention required to promote economic and human development. The central propositions of most of these studies, as summed up by Krishnamurty, were as follows: first, that the Indian economy was in a poor state of health marked by widespread poverty, lack of access to basic education and training in skills, a shortage of capital and a consequent low rate of investment; second, that Indian society was characterized by a variety of social practices that were seen as being inimical to economic development and the betterment of a wide section of people; third, while the potential for development existed, its realization would depend upon the required state support.

There was a recognition in these studies of the need to invest in education, agriculture, infrastructure and ways that would enhance the productivity of the factors of production—land, labour and capital. Specific policy interventions were identified in every sector of the economy, ranging from sanitation and public health to banking and finance, land tenure systems and rural credit to deficit finance and public investment.

In his essay 'The Present Economic Condition of India', presented to the Indian Industrial Conference at Lahore in 1909, the distinguished economist Vaman Govind (V.G.) Kale, who was later elected president of the Conference, summed up the situation in the following words:

An economic revolution is in progress in the land. The old national industries are dead and dying. New ones have not yet taken their place. The competition around us is keen and killing. We lack enterprise, capital, experience, scientific knowledge and sufficient State protection. Agriculture is in the most backward condition. Poverty and ignorance stalk over the land.[5]

Like many in his generation, Kale was deeply influenced by Japan's rise as a modern industrial nation. Indian economists also understood that for industrialization to take root in the subcontinent, local enterprise would require protection from external competition. This was a lesson learnt from the experience of all late industrializers like the Soviet Union, Germany, Japan and even the US. In his submissions to the Indian Fiscal Commission (1921–1922), one of its Indian members, Jehangir C. Coyajee, advocated a policy of 'discriminating protection' through supportive tariff rates.[6] The Fiscal Commission accepted this suggestion and laid down the criterion for such protection—that the industry securing tariff protection (a) should have a 'natural advantage', such as an abundant supply of raw material, labour, adequate power and demand; (b) would require such discriminating protection for its development; and (c) would be able to face international competition once such protection is withdrawn.

Based on such criteria, the imperial government accorded tariff protection to the Indian iron and steel industry in 1924 and, in subsequent years, to the cotton textile, cement, sugar, paper and matches industries. This finally helped reverse the phenomenon of 'de-industrialization' that European colonialism had imposed. However, on the eve of Independence, the structure of Indian industry was heavily skewed towards extractive industries producing for the global market rather than capital goods industries that could be the foundation of domestic industrialization (Table 2.1).[7]

Table 2.1: Industry-Wise Share in Net Value of Output, 1949

Industry	Percentage Share
Cotton Textiles	27
Tea	12
Jute	7
Metallurgical	6
Engineering and Electrical	5
Sugar	6
Printing and Publishing	3
Chemical	2
Tobacco	2
Others	30

Source: Cited in Bettelheim, Charles, *India Independent*, MacGibbon & Kee Ltd, London, 1968.

Recognizing the importance of State support for economic development and eradication of poverty, the Indian National Congress (INC), under the presidency of Subhas Chandra Bose, constituted a National Planning Committee (NPC) in 1938 to prepare a policy framework for India's development. The composition of the NPC is notable and shows how the leadership of the national movement viewed the priorities for planned development in a free India. It included four industrialists: Purshottamdas Thakurdas (one of the principal authors of the so-called 'Bombay Plan', which we will read about in the next chapter), Walchand Hirachand, Ardeshir Darabshaw (A.D.) Shroff and Ambalal Sarabhai; five scientists: Dr Meghnad Saha, Prof. A.K. Shaha, Dr Ahmad Nazir, Dr V.S. Dubey and Dr J.C. Ghosh; two economists: Prof. K.T. Shah and Dr Radha Kamal Mukherjee; an engineer: Sir M. Visvesvaraya; a labour leader: N.M. Joshi; and a Gandhian: J.C. Kumarappa.[8] The composition reflected the fact that there were several strands of thinking on the direction of economic policy. Mahatma Gandhi was known for his views about safeguarding cottage industries and the traditional village economy. On the other hand, Nehru was deeply committed to promoting the role of modern science and technology in economic development. Indian business leaders sought rapid industrialization. The rising labour movement sought a socialist economy.

While developments around the world, especially in Europe, Russia and Japan, significantly influenced Indian thinking on economic policy, there was a vibrant debate among Indian political and intellectual leaders about its direction. Adherents of Mahatma Gandhi's views promoted the concept of Gandhian economics, giving primacy to the village economy and the protection of traditional crafts. Socialists influenced by the impressive achievements of the then Soviet Union advocated the nationalization of private property, land reforms and public investment. The emerging Indian business leadership sought a compromise—a mixed economy in which State support would be available for private enterprise and the government would undertake land reforms, and invest in education and basic services.

3

Planning for Free India

P lanning for economic development in a free India began even before Independence. During his term as the president of the INC, Netaji Subhas Chandra Bose constituted an NPC under the chairmanship of Jawaharlal Nehru with an aim to promote industrial development.[1] A conference of provincial ministers of industries convened by the INC in October 1938 adopted a resolution stating:

> [T]he problems of poverty and unemployment, of National defence and of the economic regeneration in general cannot be solved without industrialization. As a step towards such industrialization, a comprehensive scheme of national planning should be formulated. This scheme should provide for the development of heavy key industries, medium scale industries and cottage industries, keeping in view our national requirements, the resources of the country, as also the peculiar circumstances prevailing in the country.[2]

The members of the NPC included distinguished economists, engineers, scientists, and business and political leaders. Prominent names such as Sir M. Visvesvaraya, Purshottamdas Thakurdas, Dr Meghnad Saha, A.D. Shroff, Prof. K.T. Shah, Prof. A.K. Shaha, Dr Nazir Ahmad, Dr V.S. Dubey, Ambalal Sarabhai, J.C. Kumarappa, Walchand Hirachand, Dr Radha Kamal Mukerjee and V.V. Giri were drafted to the committee. It also included representatives of the governments of Bombay, Madras, Baroda, Bihar, Hyderabad, Assam and Mysore. The NPC prepared an extensive questionnaire seeking views from across India, from experts and provincial governments, on a wide range of economic policy priorities, options and issues. It recognized the need to improve the quality of data and analysis, and the need to prioritize investment across sectors.

The NPC report identified 10 areas as the focus of planned development, including land, water, natural resources, labour, agriculture, industry, trade, credit finance and education.[3] The work of the NPC was the first systematic effort at outlining the challenge of development as well as defining the priorities for planned economic growth. The focus was clearly on industrialization.

The work of the NPC, which began in 1938, was interrupted by the Second World War and the adoption of the Quit India Resolution by the All India Congress Committee (AICC), which led to the intensification of the national movement in 1942. However, it also inspired other efforts to draft a post-Independence development plan as it became increasingly evident that India would attain freedom. The willingness of the imperial government to promote industrialization in India, also as a part of the British war effort, encouraged several

Indian leaders to prepare their charter of economic demands and plans for economic development.

The first and most promising effort was made by a group of business leaders led by Purshottamdas Thakurdas. Being a member of the NPC, Thakurdas was familiar with its initial work. He brought together India's top business leaders, J.R.D. Tata, G.D. Birla, Lala Shri Ram, as well as economists and administrators like Ardeshir Dalal and John Mathai (later a minister of finance in Nehru's first Cabinet) to put together a document that became famous as the Bombay Plan. Published in 1944, the document was titled *A Brief Memorandum Outlining a Plan of Economic Development for India*. In many ways, the Bombay Plan reflected many of the views expressed by the NPC, especially the emphasis on the role of government in promoting industrial and agricultural development, investing in education, housing and health, and infrastructure development.

The main objective of the Bombay Plan was 'to bring about a doubling of the present per capita income within a period of 15 years from the time that the plan comes into operation.'[4] It emphasized the need for public investment in the capital goods industry and power generation, and reducing dependence on foreign capital and imported consumer goods. Interestingly, the Plan did explicitly state that once the domestic private sector had come into its own and had adequate capital and capability, the government should vacate the industrial sector and allow the private sector to grow. It was probably the first time that such a case for privatization was made in India. The authors of the Plan undertook a detailed statistical analysis of the needs of the economy. They attempted to calculate the best estimates possible of the actual cash required for investment in various sectors, the actual food production necessary for the country to offer all its citizens a basic healthy diet, the output of cement, steel and other materials required to provide housing for all, the total textile production required to provide clothing for all, and so on.

The Bombay Plan was a unique document in terms of the detailed specifics it enumerated. Nowhere in the developing world had such a document been written before.[5] The interesting thing about the Bombay Plan was its focus on public investment, not just in industrial development but also in education and health. The document explicitly stated: 'The real capital of a country consists of its resources in materials and manpower, and money is simply a means of mobilising these resources and canalising them into specific forms of activity.'[6]

The Plan was based on the assumption that the government could 'create' money to finance development through deficit financing, and need not feel constrained by its current revenue-generating capacity. The Plan also recognized the need for land reforms to give the direct producer—the tiller—a stake in land improvement needed to boost the productivity of both land and labour.

The Bombay Plan was quite obviously influenced by the thinking within the NPC but it sought to distinguish itself by emphasizing the role of private enterprise and viewing the public sector as a 'transitional' necessity rather than as a permanent feature of postcolonial development. While Congress leaders like Subhas Chandra Bose and Jawaharlal Nehru, who played an important role in the NPC, placed greater emphasis on the role of the State, influenced by the successful experience of industrialization in the Soviet Union, the authors of the Bombay Plan were prominent Indian industrialists who saw domestic business as capable of playing a more significant role in economic development over time.

It is not a coincidence that independent India's First and Second Five-Year Plans (1951–1956 and 1956–1961), prepared under the guidance of Prof. P.C. Mahalanobis, a statistician, mirrored in many ways the Bombay Plan of 1944.[7] We shall discuss the Five-Year Plans in detail in the following chapters.

Let us return to the late 1940s. It was a period of considerable discussion on the future directions of economic policy in a free India. The proceedings of the NPC gave life to the many academic papers of Indian economists that we reviewed in the previous chapter. The Bombay Plan was a conscious intervention in this debate on behalf of the already highly organized Indian business community. The Federation of Indian Chambers of Commerce and Industry (FICCI), set up in 1927 on the advice of Mahatma Gandhi, had already become an influential organization advocating the views of Indian business.

It was against this background that two alternative visions of post-Independence economic policy were articulated, first by a group of socialists and second by an eminent Gandhian.

The socialist viewpoint, inspired by the socialist leader and radical humanist intellectual Manabendra Nath (M.N.) Roy, was articulated in a document authored by B.N. Banerjee, Govardhan Dhanaraj (G.D.) Parikh and Vithal Mahadeo Tarkunde and published by the Indian Federation of Labour.[8] This document, popularly referred to as the *People's Plan for Economic Development of India*, was, in fact, published

at the same time as the Bombay Plan. The opening line of
the foreword penned by M.N. Roy stated, 'The fundamental
problem of the Indian economic life is the problem of poverty.'
The document then went on to draw attention to the Soviet
experience in the interwar period and concluded that rapid
industrialization was the best way forward. The People's
Plan began its approach to industrial development from the
viewpoint of finding employment for millions of people who
were displaced from agriculture and had turned to cities for
employment. It advocated the nationalization of all natural
resources, coal and minerals. It advocated State control over
banking and finance, and extensive land reforms. Quite similar
to the Bombay Plan, the People's Plan also tried to quantify
the required investment and production in various sectors
and the role of deficit financing in enabling the government
to undertake the required investment.

Departing from traditional Soviet thinking, and perhaps
aware of some of the setbacks in Soviet industrialization,
the People's Plan ruled out the nationalization of trade in
consumer goods. India had a vibrant private sector in trade,
and this should be allowed to function rather than be taken
over by the State. The People's Plan envisaged a fourfold
increase in per capita income at the end of the first decade of
its implementation. In many ways, the Bombay and People's
plans had similar goals and emphasized the modernization
of agriculture and the pursuit of rapid industrialization. Both
emphasized the need for public investment in education and
health. Where they differed was mainly on the role of the
State. While the Bombay Plan saw only a transitional role
for government in economic development, the People's Plan
sought a more central role for the State, advocating controls

over private enterprise except in retail trade. Interestingly, both plans drew repeated attention to the Soviet experience because at the end of the Second World War and on the eve of Indian independence, the Soviet Union was viewed as a model of national empowerment through rapid industrialization.

After Gandhiji's death, it was clear to most Gandhians that, as prime minister, Nehru was bent on promoting large-scale industry, contrary to the views of Gandhiji, who had advocated the promotion of village and cottage industries. The Gandhian viewpoint on post-Independence economic policy, encapsulated in Gandhiji's vision of gram swaraj, was articulated in a booklet published in 1951 by J.C. Kumarappa. On the eve of the publication of the First Five-Year Plan, Kumarappa published his concept of what many viewed as a 'Gandhian Plan.'[9]

The Gandhian plan, however, was articulated in a very different language. While Gandhi himself did not outline any plan for economic development, his worldview was sought to be encapsulated in a document written by J.C. Kumarappa. It was published with a foreword by the eminent economist C.N. Vakil. Kumarappa defines five stages of economic development as being parasitic, predatory, enterprising, gregarious and service-oriented. A parasitic economy merely consumes without having the ability to recreate what it consumes, like a tiger killing its prey, wrote Kumarappa. A predatory economy consumes what exists without destroying the source of its consumption, like a monkey feeding off fruits from a tree. An enterprising economy creates anew but is based on available material, like a bird building its nest. A gregarious economy, like that of the honey bees, converts natural resources into new forms of consumables and stores for others' consumption. The

most evolved economic organization, concluded Kumarappa,
is one that can produce goods based on available resources but
would allow for their replenishment over time so that future
consumption needs can be supplied. This is what Kumarappa
termed a 'service' economy—an economy serving the needs
of the people as a whole.

A service economy should cater to people's basic
consumption needs and should not be producing in order
to stimulate unnecessary consumption. 'A nation cannot be
independent unless it develops self-sufficiency in its primary
needs—food, clothing and shelter,'[10] suggested Kumarappa,
advocating self-sufficiency and self-reliance even in the
development of a post-agrarian industrial economy. The
plan advocated 'co-operation' as the basis of economic
activity. It sought the end to landlordism with the direct tiller
having title to the land tilled. The village was regarded as the
relevant unit for an economic organization, with every village
community producing enough for its basic consumption.
Large-scale industry was viewed as antithetical to Gandhiji's
concept of non-violence and self-sufficiency. Kumarappa
believed: 'The idea that large-scale industries will save us is
wrong. Industrialization is only indispensable if the country's
economy is based on violence and is not calculated to meet
its daily requirements. In our country it is absolutely wasteful.
It is far too expensive for us to indulge in it.'[11]

Kumarappa's worldview would today appear far too
idealistic and utopian. His conclusion that a Gandhian
economy would be 'one which produces all that is necessary
with the co-operation of the people around for their primary
needs, viz., food, clothing, shelter, education of a type and other
public utilities brought about by the method of decentralized

control,[12] would be regarded today as impractical. However, two propositions articulated by Gandhiji have come to define contemporary economic policy in many societies. First is his theory of 'trusteeship'—that the wealthy should be trustees of wealth and care for the less privileged. It has been made part of public policy in India through the concept of corporate social responsibility (CSR) and is also captured by the idea of stakeholder capitalism. Second, Gandhiji's observation that the world has enough for everyone's needs but not enough for everyone's wants lies at the core of new thinking on sustainable and environment-friendly economic growth. The global discourse on climate change has come to accept both these Gandhian principles.

What this brief survey shows is not just that there was a vibrant debate in India and among Indians on the direction of economic policy at the time of Independence but that this debate was wide-ranging in scope, and a wide variety of views were expressed by those on the political Left, Right and in Centre. In the event, the government of free India chose a path that came closest to that outlined by the NPC and the authors of the Bombay Plan. Many of the ideas in the People's and Gandhian plans did find expression in what was termed as the Directive Principles of State Policy in the Constitution, including the promotion of village, cottage and handicraft industry, the protection of the interests of the working class, and so on. More recently, new thinking on environmentally sustainable growth and the importance of renewable energy trace their origins to Gandhian views on economic policy. Independent India benefitted from these policy debates, and successive governments gave shape to policies that continue to echo the views of the architects of free India.

4

State and the Economy

I ndia was among the first postcolonial developing
economies to adopt planning techniques to develop
a strategy of State-supported economic development.
Inspired by the experience of rapidly industrializing
economies like the Soviet Union and Japan, and Keynesian
and post-Keynesian ideas pertaining to the State's role in
economic development, India pursued post-Independence
development by drafting Five-Year Plans. Prime Minister
Jawaharlal Nehru set up the Planning Commission, acted as
its chairman and charged it with the responsibility of drafting
these plans.

The growth strategy of the First Five-Year Plan was based
on a simple model developed by economists Roy Harrod
and Evsey Domar that suggested that economic growth was
a function of investment, which, in turn, was a function of
the savings rate and the capital-output ratio, the latter being
defined as the units of capital needed to produce one unit
of output. A combination of a high savings rate and a low
capital-output ratio increased investment productivity, which,
in turn, generated higher economic growth. The Harrod–

Domar model suggested that policies aimed at increasing the investment rate by incentivizing a higher savings rate and increasing the productivity of capital would, in turn, push the growth rate up. The First Five-Year Plan document began with these words:

> The central objective of planning in India at the present stage is to initiate a process of development which will raise living standards and open out to the people new opportunities for a richer and more varied life. The problem of development of an under developed economy is one of utilising more effectively the potential resources available to the community, and it is this which involves economic planning. But the economic condition of a country at any given time is a product of the broader social environment, and economic planning has to be viewed as an integral part of a wider process aiming not merely at the development of resources in a narrow technical sense, but at the development of human faculties and the building up of an institutional framework adequate to the needs and aspirations of the people.[1]

The First Five-Year Plan aimed at increasing the share of savings and investment in the national income from 5 per cent in 1950 to 20 per cent by the mid-1960s.[2] Interestingly, even the Bombay Plan had a 15-year perspective. The First Five-Year Plan assumed a capital-output ratio of 1:3. That is, in order to produce one unit of output, three units of capital would be needed. Based on its assumptions, including population growth, the Plan forecast that per capita income would be doubled by 1977. The Plan document conceded

that this was not an ambitious target and that India could
perform better in practice.

On the issue of self-reliance and dependence on external
assistance, the Plan drew attention to two alternative examples.
The US, it argued, had developed rapidly in the interwar period
based on investment flows from Europe, while the Soviet
Union and Japan had industrialized based mainly on their
own internal resources. India, too, should try and develop
based on domestic resources, the Plan suggested, setting out
the framework for external assistance in these words:

> [E]xternal assistance is acceptable only if it carries
> with it no conditions explicit or implicit, which might
> affect even remotely the country's ability to take an
> independent line in international affairs. There are
> also obvious risks in excessive reliance on foreign aid
> which depends on the domestic political situation in
> lending countries and which might be interrupted by
> any untoward international developments. And yet,
> external resources at strategic points and stages can be
> of so much assistance in a period of rapid development
> that it is desirable, consistently with other objectives, to
> create conditions favourable to their inflow.[3]

One of the principal authors of the First Five-Year Plan, the
economist K.N. Raj, who later became a key architect of the
Delhi School of Economics and founder of the Centre for
Development Studies, Thiruvananthapuram, defined the four
key objectives of the Plan as follows:[4]

1. Double the real per capita income in the country
    by around the 1970s.

2. Reduction in the share of agriculture in the total working force from over 70 per cent in 1950–1951 to 60 per cent by the mid-1970s, while raising land and labour productivity.

3. Self-sufficiency in foodgrains and development of capital goods industries; ensure that availability of foreign exchange does not impose a constraint on development and make the country less vulnerable to external economic and political pressures; a total end to reliance on foreign aid by mid-1960s to ensure further development of the self-sustaining economy.

4. Reduction in the inequalities in income and wealth and the concentration of economic power; reduce social and political tensions associated with growth and create conditions favourable to the development of a truly democratic India.

While the First Five-Year Plan defined the broad contours of post-Independence development, it was the Second Five-Year Plan that, in fact, formalized the development strategy. In 1955, the Avadi Session of the AICC adopted a resolution stating that it would be its objective to establish a 'socialistic pattern of society' in India. This would be realized through the pursuit of 'import-substituting industrialization' and a 'mixed economy' in which the public sector would occupy the 'commanding heights' of the economy. The Second Five-Year Plan document details this objective as follows:

The socialist pattern of society is not to be regarded as some fixed or rigid pattern. It is not rooted in any doctrine or dogma. Each country has to develop according to its own genius and traditions. [...] It is

neither necessary nor desirable that the economy should
become a monolithic type or organisation offering
little play for experimentation either as to forms or as
to modes of functioning. Nor should expansion of the
public sector mean centralisation of decision-making
and of exercise of authority. In fact, the aim should be
to secure an appropriate devolution of functions and
to ensure to public enterprises the fullest freedom to
operate within a framework of broad directives or rules
of the game. [...] The accent of the socialist pattern is
on the attainment of positive goals; the raising of living
standards, the enlargement of opportunities for all,
the promotion of enterprise among the disadvantaged
classes and the creation of a sense of partnership among
all sections of the community. [...] Economic policy and
institutional changes have to be planned in a manner
that would secure economic advance along democratic
and egalitarian lines.[5]

The objectives of the Second Five-Year Plan were to seek:

1. a sizeable increase in national income so as to raise
   the standard of living in the country;
2. rapid industrialization with particular emphasis on
   the development of basic and heavy industries;
3. a significant expansion of employment opportunities;
   and
4. reduction of inequalities in income and wealth and
   a more even distribution of economic power.[6]

To attain these objectives, the State was called upon to
participate both in enhancing output and in ensuring the

equitable distribution of income. The strategy of economic development that resulted from the desire to address these objectives has been variously termed as 'mixed economy'— with a mix of public and private sectors—and 'state capitalism', in which the State was called upon to promote capitalist development. Interestingly, as we have already seen in the previous chapter, both the Bombay Plan and the People's Plan and, indeed, the NPC, headed by Nehru and Bose, emphasized the role of the State in national economic development, at least in the initial stages of development.[7]

Five-Year Plans became the principal policy instruments for State-directed economic development. The fact that Indian planning delivered results in the very first decade after Independence reinforced confidence in planned development. It was the crisis years of the 1960s, with a 'plan holiday' being declared in 1966–1969, that weakened this confidence. By the turn of the century, planned development regained momentum with achieved growth rates approximating target rates (Table 4.1).

Table 4.1: Average Annual Rate of Growth of GDP (Target and Actual)

Five-Year Plan	Period	Target Rate (in per cent)	Achieved Rate (in per cent)
First	1951–1956	2.1	3.6
Second	1956–1961	4.5	4.3
Third	1961–1966	5.6	2.4
Plan Holiday	1966–1969	–	–

Five-Year Plan	Period	Target Rate (in per cent)	Achieved Rate (in per cent)
Fourth	1969–1974	5.7	3.3
Fifth	1974–1978	4.4	4.8
Rolling Plan	1978–1980	–	–
Sixth	1980–1985	5.2	5.7
Seventh	1985–1990	5	6
Annual Plan	1990–1992	–	–
Eighth	1992–1997	5.6	6.8
Ninth	1997–2002	6.5	5.6
Tenth	2002–2007	8	7.6
Eleventh	2007–2012	8.1	8
Twelfth	2012–2015	8	8
No Plans	2015–2022	–	7

Source: Various Plan Documents, Planning Commission, India.

Note: In 1966–1969, 1978–1980 and 1990–1992 there were only annual plans. Five-Year Plans were terminated in 2014 by Prime Minister Narendra Modi.

The Industrial Policy Resolutions (IPRs) of 1948 and 1956, adopted by the Union Government, defined the framework for the relationship between the State and business. The 1948 resolution stated that 'the state must play a progressively active role in the development of industries'.[8] Apart from defence, atomic energy and railways, various basic sector industries, like steel and heavy machinery, were identified as the exclusive monopoly of the central government, with the rest of the industrial sector left open to private enterprise.

In 1956, the IPR was modified to give meaning to the AICC's objective of establishing a 'socialistic pattern of society'. The 1956 IPR stated:

> The adoption of the socialist pattern of society as the national objective, as well as the need for planned and rapid development, require that all industries of basic and strategic importance, or in the nature of public utility services, should be in the public sector. Other industries which are essential and require investment on a scale which only the State, in present circumstances, could provide, have also to be in the public sector.[9]

While the 1956 IPR expanded the role of the public sector, it also encouraged the growth of the cooperatives sector and restricted the scope for foreign investment. Over the years, this framework of industrial development strengthened the role of the State in the economy through a series of policy interventions, including a policy of industrial licencing, production and pricing controls, regulations, and so on, that empowered the bureaucracy and imposed constraints on private enterprise.

While there have been several changes to industrial policy over time, in practice, its impact on industrial development was mixed. The Industrial Planning and Licensing Policy Inquiry Committee (1967), chaired by R.K. Hazari, made two significant points reviewing the actual implementation of the policy for industrial licencing. First, it did not succeed in meeting its objective of steering investment in the industrial sector according to the objectives laid down in successive Five-Year Plans; and, second, in practice, it favoured particular business groups, particularly the Birlas, over others. The share of the industrial sector in national income, measured in terms of the share of value added in the industry as a percentage of GDP, did go up from just over 10 per cent in 1950 to over 20 per cent by 1960.

Apart from industrial and agricultural development, the Third Five-Year Plan also began to focus policy attention on reducing the wide disparity in regional development and inadequate generation of employment, especially in the industrial sectors. While both the Union and most state governments failed to prioritize agrarian reform, including land redistribution and tenancy reforms, public policy encouraged the growth of agrarian cooperatives. After living through the experience of acute food shortage in the early- to mid-1960s, the Union Government promoted the adoption of high-yielding varieties of food crops by promoting what came to be referred to as the 'Green Revolution'. The State also invested in higher education, setting up new universities and institutions in the fields of medicine, engineering and management. During this period, a major gap in Indian planning was the inadequate attention paid to universal literacy, primary school and technical education.

An interesting interpretation of the role assigned to the State in economic development was offered by a Polish economist, Michał Kalecki, who spent some time in India as an advisor to the Planning Commission. Kalecki drew attention to the limitations of a postcolonial state in promoting rapid industrialization, especially because the dominant economic groups—big business and landlords—found themselves not being in a dominant position to influence state policy. Rather, the national liberation movements made the middle class politically influential, and the 'developmental state' offered the middle class access to power through the institution of the bureaucracy. This meant that such countries would end up neither being truly 'capitalist', nor 'socialist' and would, in fact, evolve as 'intermediate regimes'.

Kalecki's concept of an 'intermediate regime' is inspired by the situation he encountered in the 1950s in postcolonial countries such as India, Indonesia and Egypt—all characterized by a large State capitalist sector, a strong 'nationalist' leadership comprising various social classes, and exhibiting anti-imperialist and anti-feudal tendencies. Kalecki postulates the case where, due to the nature of the national liberation struggles, the 'intermediate classes'—comprising lower middle classes and the rich peasantry—come to power rather than the big business or landlord classes. Such classes stand opposed, on the one hand, to the big business and landlord class and, on the other hand, to the rural and urban workers, including the poor peasants.

However, these intermediate classes have, as yet, a narrow economic base and so utilize their 'political power' gained as a result of their leadership of the national liberation struggles to gain 'independence from foreign capital', 'carry out land reform' and 'assure' continuous economic growth'. Within this Kaleckian perspective of the postcolonial society, it is suggested that the 'basic investment for economic development must therefore be carried out by the state, which leads directly to the pattern of amalgamation of the interests of the lower-middle class with state capitalism'. Kalecki visualized a 'non-capitalist' path of economic development in a postcolonial society that aims to be both more 'egalitarian' and 'stable', that is steer clear of the pitfalls of capitalism and ensure equitable development.[10]

While postcolonial India inherited an already entrenched business and landlord class, it also inherited a government staffed by the middle classes who had secured their entry into positions of power through merit-based examinations. The British creators of the Indian Civil Service (ICS) and the Indian national leadership that chose to rename it the Indian Administrative Service (IAS) viewed them as India's 'steel frame'.[11] The growth of State-owned enterprises empowered the functionaries of the State—both the permanent civil service and the political leadership. With time, a relationship of interdependence emerged between business, politics and administration that some viewed as 'state capitalism' and others as 'crony capitalism'.

India's post-Independence strategy of State-led development, creating what came to be called a mixed economy, increased the share of the public sector in national income. In the period 1950–1964, it also contributed to fairly decent economic growth rates. With a growth rate close to 5 per cent per annum, India was among the faster-growing developing economies. The setbacks and the slowdown began after the mid-1960s. A balance of payments crisis in the late 1950s, the drought years of 1965–1967, the war with Pakistan in 1965, following the 1962 border conflict with China and the 1971 liberation of Bangladesh imposed enormous costs on the economy. The State's ability to counter the negative economic effects of these developments was limited, given the increasing demands on public finances.

The planners and business leaders who conceptualized the role of the State in development did not account for the many demands that would be made on State spending that would require a diversion of funds away from productive investment. They also underestimated the burden of poverty and economic disparities, and the welfare spending this would entail. Thus, with time, public spending got diverted from industrial and agrarian development to food and other subsidies, and a range of welfare-oriented policies. While the better distribution of income is as important a policy objective as higher production, the problem with such diversion of public expenditure was the rising level of corruption in the distribution system. Prime Minister Rajiv Gandhi once famously said that no more than 15 per cent of funds allocated for welfare-oriented programmes, in fact, reached the beneficiary, with 85 per cent being absorbed along the way in administrative costs and corruption.[12]

While a government in a democracy has to devote equal attention to the production and distribution of income, the rising role of the State as a 'provider' has impacted its role as a 'producer'. Over the years, the public sector became a provider of employment rather than an efficient producer of goods. This made the public sector less competitive and, with time, in industry after industry, it was marginalized by the emergence of more competitive private sector firms.

Finally, the creation of the licence-permit-quota raj—a system under which private businesspersons had to secure government permission for setting up businesses, that specified industry-wise import quotas and in which all private investment was regulated by the State—made State intervention more of a burden than support to economic development. The NPC, the Bombay Plan and other early endorsers of State intervention in the economy viewed the government as a facilitator of, not an obstruction to, development. The bureaucratism of the licence-permit-quota raj made State intervention in industrial development a barrier to be encountered and surmounted, not support to be sought. On the other hand, some private-sector players learnt to influence government policy and benefit from it, thereby using State intervention to their advantage. This sowed the seeds of what has come to be called crony capitalism.

5

The Indian Experiment

Just as India's political leadership was inspired by ideas about economic development from around the world, economists worldwide were also inspired by India's unique experiment of pursuing economic development in a postcolonial society within the framework of republican democracy. If Jawaharlal Nehru and Subhas Chandra Bose were inspired by Japan's and Soviet Union's example of industrialization, agrarian transformation, and scientific and technological development in the interwar years of the 1920s and 1930s, even the authors of the Bombay Plan approvingly quoted the British economist A.C. Pigou to say, 'take a leaf from the book of Soviet Russia and remember that the most important investment of all is investment in the health, intelligence and character of the people'.[1]

In the new postcolonial context, India's attempt to pursue economic development within the framework of democratic governance attracted many economists from the West to study and participate in the Indian experiment. They arrived in India to teach, conduct research and offer policy advice, often as consultants to the Planning Commission. Among the earliest to arrive was none other than the Nobel Prize-winning American economist and the 'father of monetarism', Milton Friedman. Appointed as a consultant in the Union Ministry of Finance, Friedman submitted a policy memorandum to the government of India dated 5 November 1955.[2]

While Friedman was critical of the Mahalanobis model of capital-intensive industrialization and, what he called, India's 'attempt to do too much in the public sector' as well as the 'attempt to control private investment in too rigid and detailed a fashion', he was hopeful that India would be able to register a 5 per cent per annum rate of national income growth.[3] This would have been regarded as an impressive rate at the time, considering the fact that in the preceding half-century, the economy of British India grew at barely 0 per cent per annum. Friedman sought greater space for private enterprise than was being given by the policy regime of the day. His was a manifesto for a more market- and trade-based development of the economy, as opposed to the State-led model that was being pursued at the time. He was in favour of eliminating foreign exchange controls and restrictions on foreign trade.

While one could agree or disagree with Friedman's views on economic policy, he, like Pigou, also emphasized the importance of investment in health and education, echoing a view articulated in the Bombay Plan. Friedman's note began with the observation: 'The great untapped resource of technical and scientific knowledge available to India for the taking is the economic equivalent of the untapped continent available to the United States 150 years ago.'[4] The note ended with the following observation:

The fundamental problem for India is the improvement of the physical and technical quality of her people, the awakening of sense of hope, the weakening of rigid social and economic arrangements, the introduction of flexibility of institutions and mobility of people, the opening up of the social and economic ladder to people of all kinds and classes.[5]

Friedman believed that if the US had land and natural resources for the taking and its economy grew on that foundation, then India had people waiting to be deployed productively. To do so, however, India would have to first invest in the education and well-being of its millions. Many have long viewed India's population and the poverty of its people as a drag on the economy. Friedman was among the earliest to draw attention to the upside of human numbers. If these very people were properly educated, trained and converted from being social and economic liabilities into national assets, they would drive India's growth process. Investment in education and skills would be key. This was the bus that Mahalanobis and Nehru's planners missed. Rather than invest in human capital, they invested in capital goods.

Friedman was only one among an army of eminent economists who were attracted to India's experiment in democratic development. The Planning Commission, the Indian Statistical Institute and the Delhi School of Economics attracted a large number of economists from around the world, including Michał Kalecki, John Kenneth Galbraith, Paul Baran, Oskar Lange, John Strachey, Paul Streeten, Ragnar Frisch, Daniel Thorner and Wilfred Malenbaum. The eminent British economist Nicholas Kaldor was also invited to advise the Ministry of Finance on tax reform. In the US, economists like Walt Rostow and Paul Rosenstein-Rodan devoted time to the study of Indian economic policy.[6]

The intellectual contribution of these economists supplemented the high quality of domestic advice available to the government of the day from such distinguished economists as Dr V.K.R.V. Rao, Dr D.R. Gadgil, Dr K.N. Raj, Dr I.G. Patel, Dr S.R. Sen, Dr Jagdish Bhagwati, Dr Amartya Sen, Dr T.N. Srinivasan, Dr B.S. Minhas, V.K. Ramaswami, Dr A. Vaidyanathan, Dr D.T. Lakdawala, Prof. M.L. Dantwala and Dr Ashok Mitra. If these were the economists who had the ear of the government of the day, many equally distinguished economists were critical of the policies pursued at the time but whose views influenced thinking on economic policy. These included Dr P.R. Brahmananda and Dr C.N. Vakil of the Bombay School of Economics; Dr V.M. Dandekar of the Gokhale Institute of Politics and Economics, Pune; Prof. P.S. Lokanathan, the first director of the National Council of Applied Economic Research (NCAER); and Minoo Masani, one of the founders of the Swatantra Party that advocated free enterprise and opposed the Nehru–Mahalanobis model of State-led development.

What is interesting about this period was the vibrancy of intellectual debate between contending schools of economic thinking. Even though the government of the day sought to create what it called a 'mixed and a socialistic economy', it provided an environment in which conflicting views on policy were vigorously aired. Professors Brahmananda and Vakil emphasized the importance of agricultural development and the growth of labour-intensive industries in opposition to the focus on capital-intensive industrialization. Bhagwati and Srinivasan, later joined by Dr Manmohan Singh, drew attention to the importance of foreign trade and were critical of the inward orientation of the Mahalanobis strategy of import-substituting industrialization. Dr C.H. Hanumantha Rao and Dr A.M. Khusro critiqued the inadequacy of agrarian reform.

The Indian model of State-supported, postcolonial economic development was variously described as a 'mixed economy', 'bureaucratic socialism', 'state capitalism', and so on, attracting much interest in both the capitalist market economies and the centrally planned socialist economies. Indian Five-Year Plan models drew inspiration as much from the work of West European economists like Roy Harrod and Elsey Domar as they drew from East Europeans like Oskar Lange and Janos Kornai. Ideas were there for the taking, and Indian planners and policymakers drew readily from the experience of the world to build a new India.

Until the 1980s, institutions like the Indian Statistical Institute, the Delhi School of Economics and the Institute of Economic Growth were centres of vibrant policy debate among Indian economists and statisticians, and visitors from around the world. There was a proliferation of social science research centres around the country in the 1980s, contributing to state-level and decentralized planning exercises. Some of the policy debates they encouraged were ideological, between Keynesian and post-Keynesian economists, and neoclassical and Marxist economists. Some were about tactics rather than strategy, about priorities and sequencing, about the role of price signals versus that of quantitative restrictions.

If ideology played its part well, so too did vested interests and political compulsion. Economic policy in a democracy has to be politically articulated and implemented. While economists may come up with ideas, their implementation is done by elected governments. Hence, a policy is not merely a product of theory but of what is possible within a given political context. India's priority was rapid industrialization and the elimination of poverty and hunger. That India sought to achieve these goals within a democratic framework is what attracted many around the world to join hands with Indian professionals seeking to ensure the success of the Indian experiment.

Till India began its democratic journey to development, the most impressive experiments were within non-democratic frameworks. Indeed, along with India, China too began its journey to development, but within a Soviet-like one-party system. The democratic world had, therefore, a stake in India's success even though India chose a path that many in the West did not fully endorse or approve of. The difference, however, was on the instruments of policy chosen and not on the direction India's development took—as a democratic republic.

THE DISAPPOINTMENT WITH INDIA

The slowing down of the post-Independence growth process in the 1960s, which we shall examine in the next chapter, and the direction that Indian social and political life had begun to take disappointed many idealistic observers from afar. While the first two Five-Year Plans delivered against targets, subsequent plans failed to do so. It was again only after 1991 that the growth performance matched expectations.

Ideological differences between those who advocated a

continued role for the State in the economy and those who sought greater liberalization and opening up also began to emerge. Advocates of free enterprise who disagreed with Jawaharlal Nehru's emphasis on a socialistic pattern of development came together to form the Swatantra Party, under the able guidance of statesman C. Rajagopalachari and Minoo Masani and supported by business leaders like J.R.D. Tata. On the other hand, the failure to implement land reforms, slow development of employment opportunities and other persistent challenges of economic backwardness increased the appeal of communist parties.

Even as advocates of free enterprise lost interest in the India experiment because of its increasingly bureaucratic socialistic orientation, they found the export-oriented, open economy model pursued by the so-called 'Asian Tigers'— Singapore, Hong Kong, Taiwan and South Korea—both exciting and conforming to their expectations on what path newly industrializing economies ought to take. Debates raged in academic journals on the India path vs the East Asia path. By the 1980s, the interest of development economists in the West and in many developing countries turned to the East to study these 'Asian Tigers'. India's democratic credentials also became weaker and came into question when the Emergency was declared in 1975. East Asia's superior economic performance, even if within non-democratic systems, won greater appreciation. India no longer enamoured the West.

The new economic turn that India took in 1991 (discussed in Chapter 11) once again revived global interest in the Indian development model. By the 1990s, the Soviet Union had imploded and market-oriented models overtook the State-directed model of economic development. Even communist

China had opened up to trade and investment flows. A new consensus on economic policy, dubbed the 'Washington Consensus', supported and promoted by the World Bank, the International Monetary Fund (IMF) and donor countries, came to dominate development economics. China became the darling of the capitalist West, with western multinationals flooding into China. India's attraction, however, was still, as it sought to advertise at the annual World Economic Forum at Davos, Switzerland, that it was 'the world's fastest growing free-market democracy'.[7] However, as the West became increasingly wary of China's rising power, it turned to India hoping that India's now-improved performance within a policy framework of market- and business-oriented policies would offer a riposte to China. Once again, from the early 2000s, India began to attract global attention. Whether India retains this global interest in its rise will depend both on its economic performance and the political path it will adopt as it moves into the fourth quarter of its first century.

A Decade of Crises

ndependent India's economy got off to a bumpy start thanks to the country's partition. Some of the more economically better-endowed regions went to Pakistan both on the western and eastern side. The long-integrated agrarian, industrial and trading economies of the Punjab and Bengal regions were disrupted. As we have seen in the last few chapters, despite the fiscal burden of Partition and the cost of building a new republic, India's political and business leadership demonstrated the vision and courage to think long-term and create a framework of planned development. During the 1950s, India's national income (real gross domestic product) grew at an annual average rate of 3.6 per cent.[1] This compared with a near-zero rate of growth in the period before the Second World War, and compared favourably with the growth experience of the other newly independent developing economy like China.

The optimism generated by the First and Second Five-Year Plans increased the economy's appetite for new investment. Prime Minister Jawaharlal Nehru invited foreign investment, hoping it would supplement domestic public investment and contribute to building new industrial capacity. India pinned its hopes on investment from the US, the UK, Germany and Japan. While Europe and Japan were still busy rebuilding their war-damaged economies, the US private sector took little interest in India. With the domestic demand for capital goods rising rapidly, thanks to public investment, India was forced to step up imports. This contributed to a sharp drawdown of foreign exchange reserves in the first two years of the Second Plan period.

The First Five-Year Plan began with foreign exchange and gold reserves valued at $2,000 million in 1950. By 1952 these were valued at $1,729 million, and the forex position remained stable till 1956. The stepping up of industrial investment increased India's import demand and drew down forex reserves sharply from $1,814 million in 1956 to $416 million by 1958, raising alarm bells. The government of India borrowed $200 million from the IMF,[2] and an additional $350 million from a consortium of five countries—US, UK, Canada, Germany and Japan—led by the World Bank. Managing the surge in imports and sudden depletion of foreign exchange was the first major economic crisis that independent India had to deal with, apart from the economic consequences of Partition.

Despite all the challenges of a newly independent nation, the 1950s ended on a positive note. The 1960s, however, were a different story as they witnessed multiple crises. The first major shock was the border war with China. Apart from the political and geopolitical shock it administered, weakening the authority of Prime Minister Nehru, it imposed new economic burdens. The government had not devoted much attention to defence spending in the 1950s. So, it had to sharply increase spending on arms purchases. Defence expenditure as a percentage share of central government expenditure went up from 19.60 per cent in 1961–1962 to 25.50 per cent in 1963–1964. As a share of the GDP, it was up from 1.70 per cent in 1961–1962 to 3.84 per cent in 1963–1964. Over the four years, 1963–1967, defence spending exceeded 3 per cent of the GDP.[3]

Even as the government was dealing with the fiscal impact of the sudden and steep increase in defence spending, it was required to address a major crisis on the food front caused by the failure of monsoons in 1965 and 1966, triggering a major drought across the country. Agricultural production declined by 17 per cent in 1965–1966 as compared to the previous year and foodgrains production went down by a whopping 20 per cent.[4] There was no improvement in the following year. Food price inflation triggered generalized price inflation, and the government was forced to import foodgrains. The United States Agency for International Development (USAID) financed these under the PL 480 scheme, also known as Food for Peace programme. So dire was the consequence of this crisis that India was said to be leading a 'ship to mouth' existence.

The Aid-India Consortium of developed country creditors formed initially to help India with the foreign exchange crisis of 1957–1958, led by the World Bank, once again stepped in to help India deal with the food crisis. The Bank sent a mission under the leadership of Bernard R. Bell, which came to be known as the Bell Mission, with a mandate to study the Indian government's policy response to various economic challenges it was then facing and suggest policy options. Apart from strongly supporting the Green Revolution, the Bell Mission suggested India pay greater attention to agriculture and raw materials availability, reducing its emphasis on heavy industries and import substitution. The Bell Mission had also recommended devaluation of the rupee along with the elimination of export subsidies and import controls. Even as India was dealing with the consequences of the drought and recovering from a phase of political uncertainty caused by the death of Prime Minister Nehru, a war erupted between Pakistan and India, with Pakistani troops seeking to enter the Indian state of Jammu and Kashmir (J&K). India retaliated with force, widening the conflict along the border across the state of Punjab. What began as border clashes during the summer of 1965 blew up into full-blown war with a large number of tanks mobilized along the border and the Air Force also engaged in operations. The major battles were staged in September 1965 for a couple of weeks before a ceasefire was declared. While Pakistan failed in its objective of securing a grip over J&K, the war worsened the already weak economic situation. While the war came to an end, the period of political uncertainty continued with the death of Prime Minister Lal Bahadur Shastri in January 1966.

Indira Gandhi took charge as prime minister at a time when the ruling INC was buffeted by both left-wing and right-wing opposition political parties. In the Lok Sabha elections of 1962 the INC had won 361 seats in a house of 494 members. In the 1967 elections, its numbers dwindled to 283 seats. This was followed by two years of political jostling within the INC between what came to be dubbed the 'syndicate' of regionally powerful political chieftains and a ginger group of Indira Gandhi's supporters. The INC eventually split in 1969. This period of political uncertainty and internal power struggle within the ruling INC was also marked by the emergence of powerful regional political leaders and parties, like Dravida Munnetra Kazhagam's (DMK) Anna Dorai in Tamil Nadu, Communist Party of India (Marxist)'s (CPI[M]) E.M.S. Namboodiripad in Kerala, Bharatiya Kranti Dal's Charan Singh in Uttar Pradesh, and so on.

On the economic front, a major consequence of this phase of wars, drought and the consequent economic disruption was the emergence of inflationary pressures, on the one hand, and fiscal stress on the government, on the other. In the immediate post-drought years 1966–1967 and 1967–1968, wholesale prices rose sharply and the inflation rate was in double digits. To secure control over prices, the government adopted what is called a deflationary fiscal policy, requiring a reduction in the fiscal deficit, and a tight money policy, entailing higher interest rates.

To deal with the pressure on the balance of payments, the government was forced to seek foreign aid and accept the advice offered by the Bell Mission to devalue the rupee. While inflation is always a politically sensitive matter, given its adverse distributional implications, the devaluation of the rupee in June 1966, from ₹4.76 to a dollar to ₹7.50 to a dollar[5], also became a matter of serious political contention. While devaluation was accompanied by changes in export and import policy as well as a reduction in tariffs that partly neutralized the economic impact of devaluation, the issue became a political hot potato because the government's critics charged it with undertaking these policy changes under pressure from the US, the World Bank and the IMF.[6]

How did the government respond to each of these crises and what impact did the decade of crises have on the economy? The wars with China and Pakistan woke up the government to the need to step up India's defence spending. As already mentioned, there was a steep increase in the defence budget in 1963-1964 itself, immediately after the war with China. Over the next four years, the share of defence spending in total central government expenditure remained in the range of 22-25 per cent and the share of defence expenditure in the GDP remained above 3 per cent. Defence spending was eased only after 1966, following the war with Pakistan. In short, the two wars forced the government to devote a higher share of its budget and national income to defence, in turn, requiring it to reduce expenditure elsewhere. Thus, apart from the direct costs imposed by the two wars, they also imposed indirect costs by reducing spending on development and welfare programmes.

The successive droughts of 1965 and 1966 had a negative impact on food availability and consumption, government spending as well as on the balance of payments, however, they had one major positive impact too. Prime Minister Lal Bahadur Shastri tasked his minister for food, C. Subramaniam, to explore ways in which India could attain food self-sufficiency. The answer was found in what has come to be called the 'Green Revolution'. The key components of the Green Revolution were the adoption of high-yielding varieties of seeds for wheat and paddy, assured irrigation, and the use of nutrients and fertilizers to boost per acre output yield.

Prime Minister Shastri chose to give agriculture a new push with a 'new agricultural strategy' that focused on the welfare and rational economic behaviour of the farmer. Rather than get the government to procure foodgrains from farmers, Prime Minister Shastri chose to incentivize farmers by increasing agricultural prices. He created the Agricultural Prices Commission (APC), later called the Commission on Agricultural Costs and Prices (CACP), which offered 'remunerative prices'. Price incentives were combined with the introduction of the new 'green revolution' technology to enhance food production. Dealing with a war and a food crisis, Shastri gave the nation the famous slogan *'Jai Jawan, Jai Kisan* (Hail the soldier, hail the farmer)!'

An important policy consequence of this decade of crises was the decision of the Union Government to take a break from Five-Year Plans. Disrupted by war, drought and high inflation, the Third Five-Year Plan (1961–1966) failed to deliver on its promises. Then came the devaluation of the rupee in 1966. Forced to adapt policy to changing and difficult circumstances, the government took what has been described as a 'plan holiday'. The three years of plan holiday, 1966–1969 in which only annual plans were drawn up were also years of political transition. The death of Shastri, the beginning of the Indira years and the split in the Congress party provided an uncertain political context for economic policy. It was only in 1969 that macroeconomic policy was, once again, sought to be defined by a Five-Year Plan with the launch of the Fourth Five-Year Plan (1969–1974).

Two politically weak prime ministers, Lal Bahadur Shastri in his brief term in office and Indira Gandhi in her first two years in office, had to manage multiple crises, find their way through several political minefields and deal with a difficult economic situation. Indira Gandhi accepted the World Bank and US recommendation of rupee devaluation, hoping that this would be followed by increased foreign aid and investment. However, neither was forthcoming. The

Lyndon Johnson administration in the US took little interest in supporting India. Rather than increase investment, the Bank and the Aid-India Consortium reduced aid to India. There was a political backlash in India with Mrs Gandhi's critics accusing her of devaluing the rupee under western pressure without securing any benefit from it.

It was against this complex economic and political situation that Prime Minister Gandhi took a sharp turn to the Left, using the nationalization of industry and commerce as a way to weaken the alliance, as she viewed it, between her political rivals and big business. She pushed for radical land reforms to hit at entrenched feudal interests in many states that had opposed her policies. Finally, she further tightened the regime of controls and licences that gave the government even greater power over businesses. The 'decade of crises' ended in a sharp turn in India's economic policy orientation.

7

Economic Policy Turns Left

One consequence of the decade of crises was the slowing down of economic growth. After recording an annual average rate of economic growth of 4.1 per cent in 1951–1965, growth slowed down in 1965–1980 to 3.2 per cent per annum.[1] Most of this slowdown occurred during the second half of the 1960s and the 1970s. Thus, if one were to consider decadal averages, the average rate of growth of real GDP has been estimated to be 3.6 per cent for the decade 1950–1959, 4 per cent for 1960–1969 and 2.9 per cent for 1970–1979.

Buffeted on the one hand by successive economic crises and the slowdown of growth and, on the other, by political challenges posed by the divisions within the INC, its eventual split in 1969, and the rise of several non-Congress political parties, including the communists and the Jana Sangh, Prime Minister Indira Gandhi took a sharp turn to the Left in her economic policies. Her first major initiative was the nationalization of 14 private sector banks that had been estimated to be controlling 85 per cent of all deposits.[2]

The power of moneylenders and finance capital was

long recognized as an important policy challenge, both from political and developmental perspectives. Providing access to affordable finance to peasants, craftsmen and small producers was always recognized as an important policy objective even in British India. Moneylenders played a useful economic role but they were always accused of charging usurious rates of interest. The decision to nationalize the erstwhile Imperial Bank, later named the State Bank of India, was taken as part of Nehru's plan to create a 'socialistic pattern of society'. However, it was not ideology alone that drove that decision but the pragmatic view that providing access to affordable finance to all sections of society was an important policy objective.

An economic slowdown and the food crisis of the 1960s once again placed access to affordable finance at the centre of public policy. Equally, rising concerns about oligopolistic and monopolistic practices of big business houses and the fact that many of them owned private banks from which they drew funds for their businesses also necessitated a relook at banking policy. The report of the Monopolies Inquiry Commission (MIC), which was submitted in 1965, had already drawn attention to the restrictive trade practices of big business houses. There was also considerable criticism that private commercial banks were not lending enough to agriculture and small-scale industry. The government decided to play a role in influencing the credit policy of private banks. Initially, the Congress party favoured what was called 'the social control of banks'.[3] This policy was aimed at ending the control of banks by big business houses. Private banks had to appoint a board of directors with professionals and government officials, and the management of private banks was vested in professional bankers rather than business persons. Even before this experiment could deliver any results, Indira Gandhi opted for the nationalization of 14 major banks to ensure that they delivered on their social objectives of providing adequate credit to all sections of society.

The decision to nationalize banks also had a political objective in ensuring a division within the Congress, with those favouring the move uniting under the leadership of Indira Gandhi and those opposing the move, supporting its principal critic, Finance Minister Morarji Desai. The split in the Congress party ran parallel to these shifts in policy. The non-Congress opposition was sharply divided on the issue, with the Communist Party of India (CPI) supporting the Indira Gandhi government, and the Swatantra Party and Jana Sangh opposing her move.

While bank nationalization was announced in July 1969, the government secured parliamentary approval for the Monopolies and Restrictive Trade Practices (MRTP) Act in December 1969. This decision, too, was based on the views of the MIC. The government also brought in other legislation aimed at curtailing the power of big business. All business houses with assets of more than ₹200 million or controlling one-third of the production or distribution of any goods or services were prevented from expanding or diversifying their business portfolio without prior government approval. The so-called licence-permit-quota raj was further empowered.

A government committee under the chairmanship of the economist Dr R.K. Hazari, set up in 1967, had examined the working of the licencing policy and concluded that big business houses, especially the Birla Group, had, in fact, benefitted from the working of the policy and that modifications would have to be made to ensure that the policy did not favour big business. Following up on this, the government appointed a Licensing Policy Inquiry Committee to suggest policy changes. In February 1970, the government came forward with a policy that restricted the business activity of 20 large industrial houses, limiting their investments to certain 'core' industries dealing with basic and strategic sectors. The policy also reserved certain areas purely for the public sector and increased the areas reserved only for small-scale industries. It created a new concept of a joint sector in which there could be public-private partnerships.

Having curtailed the monopoly powers of finance capital through bank nationalization, the government now sought to exercise control over industrial capital. Taken together, all these changes increased governmental control of the private sector, establishing a clear leftward shift in economic policy. Indira Gandhi's focus then turned from monopoly capital to feudal landlords. In a move that hurt several erstwhile Indian rulers who were politically gravitating toward non-Congress right-wing parties like the Swatantra Party and Jana Sangh, the Congress sought to terminate the privy purses and princely privileges granted to them at the time of their incorporation into the Union Republic. The Supreme Court rejected the provisions of a Bill that the government introduced in Parliament. Following this, Indira Gandhi went into the Lok Sabha elections in early 1971, seeking popular support for her leftward tilt. Returning to Parliament with a larger mandate, she went ahead with this decision. More importantly, she relaunched the aborted land reforms programme.

Hailing the verdict of the 1971 election, the Congress party observed:

The people's verdict in the Lok Sabha elections is therefore an unambiguous mandate to the Congress to go ahead towards radical socio-economic changes to break the stranglehold of the monopoly on our economy, to take steps to raise the living standards of the downtrodden sections of society, to remove constitutional bottlenecks in the way of implementing the directive principles enshrined in our Constitution and thus to take India forward towards a progressive, socialist, self-reliant economy.[4]

The end of feudal landlordism was an important objective of the national movement and much was done to end the zamindari system in the 1950s. There were also attempts at imposing a ceiling on the land owned. Yet, over the years, the political power of landlords and rich peasants had increased. Close to 40 per cent of all ruling party members of Parliament were from landowning rural families in 1970. The Union Government convened a Chief Ministers' Conference in 1972 and encouraged them to lower land ceiling, ensure the security of tenancy and promote the notion of 'land to the tiller'. While these reforms were implemented unevenly across states, with more effective implementation in states like Kerala, J&K and West Bengal, they did further consolidate the government's leftward tilt in economic policy. We shall return to a more detailed discussion of agrarian reform in Chapter 9.

Having successfully carried out bank nationalization in 1969, Indira Gandhi undertook a series of other nationalizations after her return to power in 1971. In August 1972, the government nationalized 107 general insurance companies.[5] Following the Coal Mines (Nationalization) Act,

1973, all coal mines were nationalized. This was undertaken under the leadership of the minister for steel and mines, the late Mohan Kumaramangalam, a communist leader who joined the Congress party along with other communist leaders like K.V. Raghunath Reddy, who went on to become the minister of labour, D.P. Dhar, K.R. Ganesh, Chandrajit Yadav and Rajni Patel.[6]

The next sector to face nationalization was iron and steel. While the steel undertakings of the Tata group remained untouched, the Indian Iron and Steel Company (IISCO) was nationalized in 1972. Several other private firms in the metals industry were also nationalized. Several mills in the sugar and textiles industries too were nationalized during this period. In the case of sugar, some of the private sector mills were taken over by state governments and converted into cooperative societies. Various social objectives, ranging from the welfare of raw material producers to that of labour and even the consumer, were cited to justify these nationalizations.

Of all the experiments in nationalization, the one that proved to be a disaster was the nationalization of wholesale trade in wheat. Ensuring an adequate supply of foodgrains remained an important concern of the government through the post-Independence period, but the food shortages and the inflationary spiral in food prices that followed encouraged the political leadership to attempt a government takeover of the wheat trade in 1973. The Congress party manifesto in the 1971 general elections had indicated a commitment to 'ensure the implementation of a national policy for the distribution of food and fair prices for farmers.'[7] In pursuit of this assurance, the government nationalized wholesale trade in wheat in April 1973. It was the intention of the government to follow this up with a similar move for paddy. However, the implementation of wheat trade nationalization was thwarted by traders who brought markets to a halt. Apart from this disruption, the failure of the experiment was brought about by the sudden shortfall of foodgrains in 1972 following a weak monsoon that brought back memories of food shortages that had been forgotten since the Green Revolution. The government had not been prepared for a supply shortage which was then compounded by hoarding by private traders, and food prices shot up. Faced with the problem of food price inflation and resistance to nationalization, the government was forced to withdraw wheat trade nationalization in January 1974.

The negative experience with wheat trade nationalization brought an end to the spree of nationalizations that the Indira Gandhi government had undertaken between 1969 and 1973. As it came to exist, the state of economic affairs was best summed up by two successive presidents of the FICCI. In 1972, the president of FICCI, S.S. Kanoria, observed, 'Today the levers of power over every sector of the economy, including the financial and credit institutions, are securely in the hands of the government.'[8] A year later, his successor Madanmohan Mangaldas, observed:

> Banking, insurance, coal, major part of electricity and many other industries and trades are already in the hands of the State. In less than two decades, the capital assets of industrial enterprises in the public sector are as much as, if not more than, in the private sector, particularly after recent spate of nationalizations. The growth of the public sector has been phenomenal. And the private sector now is under the strict control of the Government.[9]

The Union Finance Ministry's annual *Economic Survey of 1975* began with the observation, 'By all accounts, the year 1974–75 was a year of unprecedented economic strains in the history of Independent India.'[10] Inflationary pressures had contributed to social tensions that manifested themselves in a series of agitations by workers and students. While pointing to global inflation and the rise in oil prices, the Survey pointed to domestic factors, especially the stagnation in food production and the consequent food price inflation, as key factors contributing to the economic crisis. The same year, Prime Minister Gandhi became embroiled in a political crisis and responded to a loss of authority by imposing the Emergency. The political changes that followed were also accompanied by a shift in economic policy as the government began to take the first steps towards economic liberalization.

8

Economic Policy Shifts Right

The 1960s, the decade of crises, ended with high inflation. In turn, the inflationary pressures that built up in the early 1970s had both economic and political consequences. Close on the heels of the failed experiment of wheat trade nationalization, came the drought of 1972. Between mid-1973 and September 1974, the annual rate of inflation peaked at about 33 per cent.[1] The inflationary impact of these on food prices was compounded by the impact of the first oil crisis that pushed up crude oil prices and increased oil import costs. This inevitably exerted strain on the balance of payments, with the current account deficit rising sharply.

Different parts of the country experienced increased strikes and protests by workers, students and even government staff. The combination of high inflation and a balance of payments crisis narrowed policy options. This period of high inflation and political unrest culminated in the imposition of the Emergency in June 1975.[2] Of course, the emergency was not introduced only in response to an economic crisis but, more importantly, as a response to a political crisis arising out of renewed challenges to Indira Gandhi's leadership and her concern about external interference in India's domestic affairs.

Interestingly, the government's strong policy response to inflation, contributing to a rapid and sharp decline in the price level, had a significant impact on the professional standing of the then chief economic advisor, Dr Manmohan Singh. Prime Minister Gandhi was deeply impressed by his advice, which she followed to vigorously use fiscal and monetary policy to fight inflation and alter inflationary expectations. Freezing wage and salary increases, the freeze on 50 per cent of dearness allowance payments, an increase in rail fares, and other direct and indirect tax measures had a salutary impact on inflation that also stirred political trouble. The government used its emergency powers to come down heavily on all forms of protest and trade union activity and curtailed freedom of speech by censoring the media. Leaders of major opposition political parties were incarcerated in jails.

The fiscal consolidation measures were accompanied by monetary policy measures, including raising the cash reserve ratio, the statutory liquidity ratio and the bank rate.[3] This combination of fiscal policy and monetary policy had a deflationary impact on the economy. As for the problem with the balance of payments, India borrowed from the IMF and also drew additional aid from the Aid-India Consortium. The gradual increase in dollar remittances from an ever-increasing Indian diaspora worldwide, especially in the Gulf, helped improve the foreign exchange position. The depreciation of the rupee helped boost exports and curb imports, and further reduced the current account deficit.

The government introduced a series of changes in industrial policy aimed at liberalizing it. In several industries, the industrial licencing policy was eased. Firms were given a greater degree of freedom in making investment decisions, expanding capacity and raising asset limits on the small-scale industry. In their assessment of economic policy during this period, authors Vijay Joshi and I.M.D. Little take the view that exogenous factors like good monsoon and increasing foreign exchange remittances played their part, along with domestic policy intervention, to stabilize the economy. Hoping this positive economic situation would win popular support, Prime Minister Gandhi lifted the Emergency and called for fresh elections to the Lok Sabha. She was defeated and her former colleague who had opposed her leftward turn in economic policy, Morarji Desai, led the first non-Congress government in New Delhi.

Desai was a Gandhian but pro-business, a critic of Nehru's and Indira Gandhi's 'socialistic' policies and vehemently opposed bank nationalization. He was also a fiscal conservative who did not believe in 'big' government. His finance minister, H.M. Patel, was a retired member of the ICS, also known for his economic policy conservatism. One of their earliest decisions was to appoint a committee to examine the regimes of controls and subsidies under the chairmanship of another fellow Gujarati, Vadilal Dagli, a writer, poet and an economist with a doctoral degree from the University of California at Berkeley. He served as the financial editor of *The Indian Express* and became the editor of a business and finance journal, *Commerce*. The Dagli Committee on Controls and Subsidies (1979) reviewed all governmental controls on economic activity in place from British India and those imposed after Independence and recommended a comprehensive review to eliminate all redundant regulations and controls. However, the thrust of the report was on rationalizing, simplifying and minimizing controls rather than their elimination. It was only in the 1980s that a wider consensus began to emerge in favour of what the economist Dr I.G. Patel famously termed a 'bonfire of controls.'[4] However, that bonfire was to be lit a decade later, in 1991, by Prime Minister P.V. Narasimha Rao.

While the short-lived Morarji Desai government did not take too many radical policy steps and, given the fragile nature of the political coalition, could do little to improve the fiscal balance, it nevertheless brought to an end the leftward shift in economic policy. One area in which reform was initiated was trade policy. In 1978, a committee chaired by commerce secretary P.C. Alexander recommended easing import restrictions with imports classified under three heads—banned, restricted and open general license. Finally, the exchange rate policy aimed to set exchange rates at more realistic, market-relevant rates. Taken together, a series of trade-related policy changes liberalized the external trade regime.

Interestingly, Indira Gandhi herself finally initiated a faster-paced shift towards a more liberal and business-friendly economic regime when she returned to office in 1981. Opting for an extended fund facility (EFF) loan from the IMF, Mrs Gandhi not only signalled a willingness to undertake policy reform at home but also to improve relations with the IMF's biggest shareholder, the US. A new Industrial Policy Statement was issued in July 1980, further liberalizing provisions relating to licencing, capacity expansion, and import of machinery and utilization of foreign exchange. Large corporate entities covered by provisions of the MRTP Act, 1969 and the Foreign Exchange Regulation Act (FERA), 1973, were offered more freedom to expand capacity and utilize foreign exchange, and the telecom sector was opened up for private investment.[5]

While Left parties and left-wing economists were concerned that the IMF loan would require the government to undertake radical policy reform in the fields of fiscal, trade and industrial policy that would have negative consequences for growth, welfare and external dependence, their critics regarded these concerns as unduly alarmist, given that the loan conditionality did not require rupee devaluation or any major policy reset apart from what the government of the day had already decided to do. Policy reform focused on fiscal correction and balance of payments management necessitated by a sharp increase in oil prices in the late 1970s.

The liberalization of industrial policy, taken together with the Indira Gandhi government's new approach to economic policy, did positively impact what economists call the 'animal spirits' of private enterprise. Not only did new business groups like the Ambanis enter business and grow rapidly, but the manufacturing sector grew at a fast pace of 7.7 per cent, with the registered manufacturing sector growing by a whopping 11 per cent, in 1982–1985. Joshi and Little attribute this growth to an increase in domestic demand, public investment in infrastructure and what they call, 'the tilt toward liberalization'.[6]

The Rajiv Gandhi government took the process of industrial policy liberalization further forward. Steps taken during the late 1970s to facilitate industrial capacity expansion to improve economies of scale and factor productivity, and boost exports were built upon. Most of these measures were incremental, making it easier for big firms to grow bigger. More importantly, they signalled a change in approach to industrial and finance capital. The lack of trust and hostility that defined the aggressive nationalization and licence-permit-quota raj phase of the early 1970s was replaced by a reaching out to big industry. After taking charge as prime minister, Rajiv Gandhi appointed several prominent business leaders as chairpersons or board members of public sector enterprises. This included Ratan Tata as the chairman of Air India and Rahul Bajaj as the chairman of Indian Airlines. Former ITC chairman, the late Yogi Deveshwar, Russi Mody, Arun Nanda, Vivek Bharat Ram, Pratap Reddy, and others were invited to oversee various public enterprises.

While this experiment of managing public enterprises with talent from the private corporate sector did not succeed in vastly improving public enterprise performance, it was an important policy signal that indicated a changed attitude to private enterprise. Rajiv Gandhi distanced himself from his grandfather's and his mother's 'bureaucratic socialism' and opened up the economy to private enterprise. His administration also focused policy attention on the development of the information technology and communication industries, pushing for computerization of public services.

The government appointed several committees of experts and officials to review industrial, trade and financial sector policies and recommend ways to further reduce the scope of the licence-permit-quota raj. That a new consensus was emerging among policymakers on the need for economic liberalization was emphasized by a highly regarded member of the erstwhile policymaking community, Dr Patel. He was the Union Government's chief economic advisor in the early to mid-1960s and served as secretary of economic affairs in the Union Ministry of Finance during Indira Gandhi's first few years in office. He was appointed governor of the Reserve Bank of India (RBI) by Morarji Desai and completed his term after Mrs Gandhi's return to office in the early 1980s. In 1987, he delivered a landmark lecture in Cambridge, UK, titled 'On Taking India into the Twenty-First Century.' Dr Patel was forthright:

> Even those of us who had actively promoted the earlier policies of the 'fifties and the early 'sixties have come to realise for some time now that we had underestimated the long-term deleterious effects of controls and had not appreciated sufficiently the potential for a self-serving alliance between political leaders and civil servants, on the one hand, and captains of industry or the large farmers who have sufficient clout both socially and financially, on the other.[7]

Dr Patel reflected the thinking of a wide section of policymakers at the time. However, the changes made to extant policy till 1990 were essentially incremental. In 1989, Prime Minister Vishwanath Pratap (V.P.) Singh had asked an official in the prime minister's office, Montek Singh Ahluwalia, to draft a note on policy reform, and many of his ideas found their way into proposals for economic reform authorized by his successor Prime Minister Chandra Shekhar Singh. However, only few of these ideas could be translated into policy till Prime Minister P.V. Narasimha Rao finally authorized a regime change in economic policy in July 1991.

Even the gradual pace of incremental economic reform

undertaken in the 1980s had a positive impact on economic growth. The major structural transformation in the economy had happened first in agriculture thanks to the Green Revolution. This itself had pushed up macroeconomic growth. Industrial sector reform further contributed to an acceleration of economic growth. As a consequence, the average annual GDP growth rate went up from 3.5 per cent in the period 1950–1980, to 5.5 per cent in the following decade. The 1980s also saw a dispersal of industrial activity away from the traditional centres like Maharashtra, Tamil Nadu and West Bengal to new regions like Gujarat, Karnataka and Andhra Pradesh.

The downside of this positive story of the 1980s was the worsening of the Union Government's fiscal position, especially during Rajiv Gandhi's tenure. Joshi and Little observed:

> The major mistake of macroeconomic policy lay in neglecting the danger signs evident in 1985-86 on the fiscal front. Fiscal deterioration was allowed to proceed apace. As a consequence, the current account deficit continued to worsen and domestic and foreign debt continued to increase at a dangerous rate. By the end of the decade, the macroeconomic fundamentals were out of joint. Even a strictly temporary shock like the Gulf War was enough to trigger a full-scale crisis.[8]

In short, while Rajiv Gandhi pioneered considerable economic reform and modernization of the economy, and the governments of his immediate successors, V.P. Singh and Chandra Shekhar Singh, were willing to take the process forward, fiscal mismanagement by both Rajiv Gandhi and

V.P. Singh, created the domestic conditions for an external payments crisis. While the oil shock and other effects of the Gulf War acted as triggers, five years of irresponsible fiscal management had prepared the ground for a balance of payments crisis. We shall return to an examination of the economic crisis and reforms of 1991 in Chapter 11.

Changes in the Agrarian and Regional Landscapes

Seventy-five years have passed since industrial development gained pace, but agriculture remains the mainstay of the Indian economy. Though the sector today accounts for only 20 per cent of national income (GDP), reduced from 55 per cent in 1950; 58 per cent of the population and 70 per cent of all rural households remain dependent on agriculture for their livelihood. While landlords and rich peasants may dominate policymaking in the sector, 82 per cent of those engaged in agriculture are small and marginal farmers. Indian agriculture has come a long way from the era of 'enforced commercialization' during the interwar period and the 'ship-to-mouth'[1] existence of the drought-hit mid-1960s. India is self-sufficient in foodgrains production, although many go hungry due to a lack of purchasing power or access to food. According to the Food and Agricultural Organisation (FAO), India is the largest producer of milk, pulses and jute and the second-largest producer of wheat, rice, sugarcane, cotton, groundnuts, and fruits and vegetables.[2]

Yet, rural poverty and unemployment abound, making the Mahatma Gandhi National Rural Employment Programme (MGNREGP) a sought-after service of the government. Success in stepping up agricultural output but lack of success in reducing the dependence on the agricultural economy for one's livelihood, and persistent poverty and hunger is the paradox of agrarian change in India.

India's early planners and policy thinkers understood the importance of these challenges. The First Five-Year Plan identified an increase in agricultural production as 'the highest priority in planning over the next few years' and recognized the need to diversify crop mix, land use, production efficiency and rural infrastructure. The planners emphasized the need to develop cooperative institutions that would enable farmers to pool their resources and overcome the handicap of the small size of farms. They also impressed upon the need for the government to offer extension services that would help farmers secure access to better quality seeds and new technologies that would improve farm productivity and farmers' incomes. The Bombay Plan, discussed in an earlier chapter, also identified the uneconomic size of farms, rural indebtedness, soil erosion, access to water and low yields per hectare as some of the challenges. Both plans recognized the need to ensure that agricultural commodity prices are both remunerative and stable. Hence, there was a consensus built around an agrarian strategy that would seek to improve the productivity of agriculture, undertake some institutional reform and promote public investment in necessary infrastructure.

Interestingly, while the First Five-Year Plan identified the pattern of land ownership as a policy concern, it naively advocated the need to bring together the 'village community' in order to implement government policies. The document did recognize the different economic interests of various categories, namely, 'intermediaries, large owners, small and middle owners, tenants-at-will and landless workers.' The plan document very correctly stated:

> The future of land ownership and cultivation constitutes perhaps the most fundamental issue in national development. To a large extent the pattern of economic and social organisation will depend upon the manner in which the land problem is resolved. Sooner or later, the principles and objectives of policy for land cannot but influence policy in other sectors as well.[3]

Both the First Five-Year Plan and the Bombay Plan emphasized the need for land reform and to empower the tiller and the tenant, as opposed to the landlord and the zamindar. The Bombay Plan summed it up well when it said:

> Along with the development of cooperative farming and irrigation, prevention of soil erosion and water-logging, afforestation, etc, a fundamental reform which is necessary, if the target for agricultural production is to be reached and if the income of the cultivator is to be raised, is the reform of the land system.[4]

So what was this land system? India presented a differentiated system of land ownership and tenure at the time of Independence. While feudalism remained entrenched in many parts of the country, giving zamindars, jagirdars and other feudal landowners control and power over land, change was afoot in other parts, where owner cultivators were emerging as rich peasants. British India was defined by two systems of revenue settlement—zamindari and ryotwari. In many Indian states, like Hyderabad, the zamindari system prevailed. In areas under zamindari settlement, mainly in the Bengal Presidency and Bihar, the intermediary between the peasant and the State had little incentive to invest in improving the land or its tiller. In areas defined by what was called the ryotwari settlement, mainly the Madras and Bombay Presidencies, the peasant proprietor had an incentive to invest in the land and improve his lot.

Once India became independent, the landed elite used the institutions of democracy to retain their economic power, and their social and political influence. There was a constituency for land reform in the national movement, but it was divided between moderates and radicals. Acharya Vinoba Bhave, a Gandhian from Maharashtra, was a moderate who campaigned for voluntary land alienation by the landlords. He led the Bhoodan Movement—also known as the Land Gift Movement—to convince the feudal landlords that it was in their best interest to part with a portion of their estate and transfer the land to the tenants—the peasants who tilled the land. On the other end, there were the communists who advocated an armed struggle and forced seizure of land from the feudal landowners. The present-day state of Telangana, which was then part of Andhra Pradesh, was home to one of the largest armed struggles of the communists. Standing between the moderates and the radicals, Jawaharlal Nehru opted for a compromise. The feudal system of revenue collection instituted by the colonial state system was abolished, security of tenure was sought to be ensured and the State provided access to credit and other forms of institutional support to the peasant.

There have been three elements to the Indian understanding of land reforms: first, abolition of absentee landlordism; second, a ceiling on total landholding aimed at freeing 'surplus' land for redistribution; and, third, ensuring security of tenancy. While the first was implemented to a great extent in most parts of the country, the second was subverted through large landowners carving up their estates in the name of not just family members but also their dogs and horses. The third reform has been more successfully implemented with time.

While feudal landlords retained some of their economic and social power and authority, democratic politics increasingly empowered the rich peasants—dubbed 'bullock capitalists' by political scientists Susanne and Lloyd Rudolph in their classic treatise on Indian political economy, *In Pursuit of Lakshmi*.[5] Many zamindars and jagirdars survived land ceiling and tenancy laws, mainly by evading them and managed to retain sizeable lands as well as their inherited social and political influence. Members of the middle peasantry were able to increase their land holdings as well as their political influence to emerge as 'bullock capitalists'—self-employed, independent cultivators. 'The balance of power between these groups,' the Rudolphs concluded, 'lay with landlords in the sixties but in the seventies it shifted towards bullock capitalists and backward classes.'[6]

The Rudolphs saw bullock capitalists emerging as the 'hegemonic agrarian class,'[7] considering their share of both land and population across the country and also, more importantly, their social and political clout. Hailing not just from upper castes but also the numerically larger middle castes—or 'backward classes' in Indian political parlance—

the bullock capitalists were set to grow in importance as members of the rural power elite.

Two important developments of the 1970s shaped the dynamics of power in rural India.[8] First, the Green Revolution, and second, the emergence of rich peasants as powerful politicians in different parts of the country. The economic enrichment and empowerment of the middle and rich peasants was an important consequence of the Green Revolution—the adoption of high-yielding varieties of food crops. Their political empowerment was ensured by their proliferation and subsequent domination of the political leadership of the ruling Congress party at the state level in almost all major states.

It was widely recognized that the Indian commercial banking system had neglected the financial needs of the peasantry and, being controlled by metropolitan big business houses, had an urban industrial bias. Between 1951 and 1961, the share of the agricultural sector in the total credit issued by private commercial banks remained static at 2 per cent while that of the industrial sector had doubled from around 34 per cent in 1951 to 67 per cent in 1967. It was partly in recognition of this static credit rate in the post-Green Revolution era that Indira Gandhi nationalized private commercial banks in 1969, ostensibly to make more credit available and accessible to farmers. Most farmers were still dependent on traditional moneylenders and local landlords who not only charged usurious rates of interest but also used defaults on such lending to acquire land from the debtor.

Apart from nationalizing commercial banks and instructing them to open new branches in rural areas and lend more to the farm sector, the government promoted the growth of several rural credit institutions, many of which came under the control of politically powerful agrarian classes. The post-Green Revolution period brought into sharp relief the growing clout of the surplus-generating rich peasant class, especially in agriculturally prosperous states like Punjab, Haryana, Andhra Pradesh and Tamil Nadu.

The economist Dr Ashok Mitra wrote eloquently about how the rising surplus-generating kulak class had acquired decisive influence on the central government's agriculture pricing policy in the post-Green Revolution period. 'The State is hardly a neutral entity. It reflects the concentration of power and authority. This authority can be directly deployed for affecting the terms of trade between classes,' wrote Mitra in his treatise on how the state manipulates terms of trade between agricultural and industrial produce to benefit surplus generating rich farmers—the rural oligarchy, as he called them.[9]

An important rural reform and development initiative taken during the First Five-Year Plan was the community development programme, partly inspired by Gandhian views on village economy and partly by new international thinking on development. Introduced in India in 1952, this initiative was supported by the United Nations (UN). The aim was to introduce village-level programmes for the improvement of the rural economy covering areas including cultivation practices, healthcare, education, infrastructure, and so on. An entire state- and district-level development administration was created to push this initiative forward, but little progress was made, at least partly due to the inherent class and caste divisions in rural society and the economy.

In her radical phase in the late 1960s, Indira Gandhi

invited the highly regarded economist K.N. Raj to chair a committee tasked to examine the possibility of levying a tax on agricultural wealth and income. The Raj Committee recommended that an agricultural holdings tax replace the existing system of land revenue. It would mimic the urban economy's income tax despite not exactly being a tax on income. Instead, the tax would be levied on the *presumed* income of a holding in different agro-climatic regions. In 2016, farmers with more than four hectares of land constituted just about 4 per cent of the total farming families, but they were estimated to account for 20 per cent of total agriculture income. One estimate showed that as much as ₹25,000 crore could be collected from these farmers if their income was taxed at 30 per cent.[10] The Raj Committee recommendations got buried thanks to political opposition from the rural land-owning classes who dominated most state assemblies across the country, and the idea of a direct tax on agricultural income has never been pursued since.

The emphasis that the First Five-Year Plan placed on agriculture was forgotten during the Second Five-Year Plan period, partly because of the focus on rapid industrial development. Neither were land reforms undertaken, nor did initiatives like community development programme succeed. Only after the food crisis of the 1950s did the rural economy once again get some policy attention. The shift in terms of trade in favour of agriculture in the late-1960s and through the 1970s had its own impact on rural incomes and on the generalized price level. Since then, much of the focus on rural and agrarian development has remained primarily on prices, credit availability, and cost and input subsidies.

Consequently, the agrarian economy remains trapped in

a low-level equilibrium in which there is adequate production but at costs that require public subsidies to enable the poor to access the supply, and where even when producers secure remunerative prices, they have become dependent on input subsidies. Taken together, these subsidies impose a huge burden on public finances. They also encourage uneconomic use, often with harmful consequences, of subsidized inputs like electricity, water and fertilizers.

REGIONAL VARIATIONS IN AGRARIAN CHANGE

Given India's continental dimensions and its regional history, it is only to be expected that different parts of the country would not only have very different agro-climatic conditions and hence, agrarian economies, but also that the different systems of revenue mobilization, under different systems of government would also have their impact on regional patterns of development. So, quite naturally, some parts of India have experienced higher rates of growth and development than others. The regional differentiation in agrarian change and development in post-Independence India has a pre-Independence history.

Regions characterized by the zamindari system and with permanent land revenue settlement experienced lower rates of productivity and income increase and, consequently, growth because public investment in such regions remained low. The government had little incentive to invest in irrigation and other rural infrastructure because any improvement in the farmer's income as a result of such public investment did not automatically translate into higher revenue for the government. Such regions could be under British rule, as in Bengal and Central Provinces, or under Indian feudal landowners, as in Gwalior. On the other hand, in regions with a temporary revenue settlement—the ryotwari system—the local government would derive an increase in its revenues as farmers' income rose thanks to public investment. This was the case in parts of western and southern India. As a result, investment in irrigation by the state in these regions contributed to an increase in output, incomes and revenues.

Thanks to this difference in revenue settlement systems, the agrarian economy of the regions with the ryotwari system developed faster. In the period 1890–1940, this regional differentiation in agricultural and industrial growth contributed to the faster development of western and southern India as compared to eastern and central India. So entrenched has this regional pattern been that even 75 years after Independence, the states of Gujarat, Maharashtra, Karnataka, Tamil Nadu and Andhra Pradesh remain the more developed regions of the country. Equally, Bihar, Madhya Pradesh, Rajasthan and Uttar Pradesh (once referred to as the BIMARU states) remain among the less developed states.

Noting a link between agrarian systems, agricultural development and regional growth, economist Dr Krishna Bharadwaj observed:

> In certain parts of Andhra Pradesh, Kerala and Karnataka in the south, Haryana in the north, and Gujarat and parts of Maharashtra, [that] have shown prominently dispersed growth[...] We note the importance of agricultural surpluses in adequate quanta to sustain industrial expansion. The regions sharing some industrial vitality appear to be the ones where agricultural growth has also been promising.[11]

Indeed, the performance of the agricultural economy has been an important determinant of the overall economic development across the subcontinent. The authors of the Second Five-Year Plan did not adequately appreciate this link and focused mainly on industrialization. The country paid the price for this unbalanced development in the 1960s, and it was only in the post-Green Revolution era that the agricultural economy began to gain momentum.

One region that benefitted as a consequence was the National Capital Region (NCR) around the country's capital city, Delhi. While Punjab, Haryana and western UP have done well due to the Green Revolution, New Delhi's expansion and the benefits of proximity to it have facilitated the industrialization and overall development of the entire NCR and its hinterland. However, despite the agrarian economy of this region developing well, the rapid growth of the urban economies has contributed to a sense of alienation from this development process, even among the rich peasants of the region. The farmers' agitation in 2020–2021, opposing reform of agriculture marketing system and seeking legal assurance for minimum support price was a manifestation of this alienation.

Indian agriculture today confronts a paradox of bountiful output and the social and economic backwardness of the rural economy. Migration from villages to towns and cities has not only hastened urbanization but has also contributed to the overgrowth of urban slums. On the other hand, it has deprived the rural economy of the educated young manpower it needs to modernize the farm sector and derive the benefits of commercial farming, as also the growth of agro-processing and processed foods industries that require skilled manpower.

What Indian agriculture and the rural economy need is better infrastructure in the form of power supply, roads, schools and colleges, public health and hospitals, and cold food chains and links to the urban and global economies. President Dr A.P.J. Abdul Kalam summed it up brilliantly in his formulation, PURA—Providing Urban Amenities to Rural Areas (the Hindi word 'pura' translates to 'wholistic'). President Kalam believed that if both soft and hard infrastructure in rural areas were of the same quality as is available in urban areas, not only would there be an improvement in the quality of life in rural areas but the economy as a whole would benefit from higher growth, better income distribution, and faster economic and social development.[12]

Towards Industrialization

The promotion of rapid industrialization has been an important objective of economic policy since Independence. Sir M. Visvesvaraya's call, 'Industrialize or perish!' became the watchword of planning. The focus of the First and, more importantly, Second Five-Year Plans was on industrial development. Industrial policy was intimately linked to trade policy because, from the early days of planned development, India opted for a strategy of what is called 'import-substituting industrialization'.

The complaint of both political and business leaders during the national movement was that the British imperial government had not provided an environment conducive to the local Indian enterprise and had allowed cheap imports to 'deindustrialize' whatever little industry that had flourished in colonial India. During the interwar period, the British government extended limited tariff protection to a few industries, including sugar and jute, mainly to prevent imports from non-British territories. As a result, there was some industrial growth, especially during the 1930s. The Second World War also helped boost industrial production in

India both because imports were disrupted and war demand had to be met.

INDUSTRIAL POLICY

We have already discussed the many debates around industrial policy and the role of Japanese and Soviet industrialization experiences in influencing the policy thinking of Indian national and business leaders. In pursuance of ideas that had taken shape in the NPC and also articulated by the Bombay Plan, the government came forward with the Statement on Industrial Policy (SIP) in 1945. It clearly stated that in 20 key industries, the government would have to invest in case adequate private investment was not forthcoming. The first important industrial policy statement of a newly independent India was adopted by Parliament in April 1948. As part of its emphasis on state investment in industry as a necessary requirement to speed up the pace of industrialization, IPR 1948 drew up a list of industries reserved for the public sector and a list of sectors open to private investment. Six sectors were reserved exclusively for the State to invest in. These included coal, iron and steel, aircraft manufacturing, shipbuilding, manufacture of telecom and other communication equipment, and mineral oils. Another 18 industries were identified as sectors in which both the public and private participation was encouraged, but State regulation and control would ensure that national requirements are met. These 18 included automobiles and tractors, salt, electric engineering, sugar, cement, paper, machine tools, textiles, air and sea transport, defense industries and so on.

In order to implement IPR 1948 and promote industrial

development, the government enacted the Industries (Development and Regulation) Act (IDRA), 1951. The Act established the policy framework for licencing and regulation of firms. No new industrial enterprise could be established without the investing firm securing a licence from the Union Government. Such a licence would specify the size of the unit, its location and so on. The IDRA 1951 also provided for the government takeover of private enterprises if the latter did not fulfil all the provisions of the licence granted. Among the many objectives of industrial policy, the key ones were that industrial establishments should meet planned targets that may be set for them; that concentration of economic power and monopolistic and oligopolistic practices would be prevented and, if necessary, penalized; small-scale manufacturers would be protected and certain sectors would be reserved for them; while new enterprise would be encouraged, the dispersal of new establishments across the country would be promoted; and, finally, new technology development would be stimulated.

One consequence of the IDRA 1951 was that it centralized industrial policy in the hands of the Union Government. Even state governments had to secure central government approval to establish an industrial unit. The government took one bureaucratic step further when it created the office of the director general of technical development that would examine the technology being sought to be deployed by any industrial licence applicant. Another consequence of this rigid licencing policy was that it eliminated competition between firms. Moreover, in practice, it was never clear to anyone as to why one particular applicant secured a licence and why someone else did not. Given the arbitrary nature of the system, businesspersons who knew how to manipulate it succeeded in securing more licences.

Not satisfied with the extent of state control on industry specified by the IPR 1948 and the IDRA 1951, the Union Government came forward with another statement in 1956 that emphasized the role of industrial policy in attaining the larger political objective of establishing a 'socialistic pattern of society'. It also prioritized the development of a capital goods industry in keeping with the Second Five-Year Plan model. The Plan underlined the need for India to free itself of dependence on capital goods imports and highlighted the need for domestic investment in the sector. The IPR 1956 increased the number of sectors reserved exclusively for public sector investment including antibiotics and other essential drugs, dyestuffs and plastics, and so on. However, in an interesting twist, the IPR 1956 also recognized that public and private sector firms could coexist in various sectors and advocated the growth of both types of firms. Hence, some critics believed that the 'socialist' rhetoric of the IPR 1956 was just a camouflage that enabled the government to take a more liberal approach in practice to the private sector.[1]

In practice, India acquired a 'mixed economy' in which the public sector, which was meant to 'occupy the commanding heights of the economy', retained a dominant position till the 1980s. The licence-permit-quota raj that came into existence made the business of manufacturing cumbersome, but because of tariff protection and the policy of import-substitution, there was some growth of private enterprise. The basic and capital goods industries increased their share of industrial output from around 27 per cent in 1956 to 47.5 per cent by 1970. By 1970, a bulk of the value-added in manufacturing was in the food and textiles industry (36.3 per cent), with metal-based products accounting for a share of 26.9 per cent. The share of manufacturing in the GDP went up from 10 per cent in 1950 to 14 per cent by 1962, the last year of the Second Five-Year Plan period. It remained at around that level for almost the next decade and a half, rising once again only in the mid-1970s and touching a peak of 17 per cent in 1978–1979. It has since then hovered around 16 per cent over the past four decades.

INDUSTRIAL GROWTH

The stagnation in the share of manufacturing in the GDP between the early 1960s and the late-1970s was a reflection of a decline in industrial output and reduced capacity utilization of existing plants. The slowdown in industrial growth from the mid-1960s till the 1980s has been explained in different ways by several economists. Some attributed this to reduced demand for manufactured goods on account of a rise in food and commodity prices, contributing to a shift in terms of trade in favour of agriculture and against manufacturing. This meant a greater share of household income was going towards paying for food and less to manufactured goods. This demand-side explanation was also made by those who saw public investment declining as a result of pressures on the government to spend less on new investment and more on subsidies, as well as the fact that poverty was pervasive, employment growth inadequate and, therefore, the home market was not growing fast enough to fuel industrial growth.

An alternative hypothesis forwarded was based on a critique of the import-substitution strategy that neglected the demand potential of the global market. It was argued that there was no reason for industrial growth to be constrained by the size of the home market if it could cater to the export market. By curtailing trade through protectionist tariffs and a variety of non-tariff barriers, government policy prevented the domestic industry from tapping the global market. This view, first put forward by economists Prof. Jagdish Bhagwati, Prof. Padma Desai and Prof. T.N. Srinivasan, gained traction in the 1980s when many East and Southeast Asian economies overtook India on the industrial front by successfully exporting manufactured goods to the world market. In India, the share of exports in the GDP, in fact, went down between 1950 and 1965 from 6.1 per cent to 2.9 per cent. On the other hand, the share of imports in the GDP remained static at around 6 per cent through this period.

In the 1950s, there was a good case for pursuing import-substituting industrialization, both because of the prevailing dominant view about foreign trade shaped by the colonial experience and because Indian industry was still in an 'infant' stage, in terms of size, scale and technical competence. But by the 1980s, the industry was on a surer footing and India was beginning to pay the price for neglecting the export potential of the economy, given that countries like South Korea and Malaysia were taking off economically, riding on the opportunities offered by the global market.

India faced its first balance of payments crisis in the late 1950s when the liberal import of capital, intermediate and consumer goods depleted foreign exchange reserves without a significant step up in exports. Faced with a foreign exchange shortage, the government was forced to impose import controls and regulations that did little to promote exports. In any case, throughout this period, exports were viewed mainly as a means of financing imports and not as an 'engine of economic growth'. The view that exports could promote overall economic growth gained currency only after the newly industrializing economies of East and Southeast Asia recorded phenomenal economic growth by building export-oriented economies. The debate among economists and policymakers about the relative importance of the home or domestic market and the export market for industrial growth, went on through the 1980s even as India's share of world trade stagnated at 0.5 per cent in the period 1960–1990. It was only in 1991 that new thinking on the role of foreign trade began to define industrial policy.[2]

The gradual increase in domestic demand, particularly after the benefits of the Green Revolution and minimum support prices that went to farmers whose consumption began to go up, and also an increase in public spending by the government began to pull up the industrial growth rate in the 1980s. The decade was also associated with a more liberal trade policy. Thus an expansion in both the home market and exports enabled an acceleration of industrial and overall economic growth in the 1980s. It was a decade of gradual change both in policy and performance on the industrial and trade fronts. After a decade and a half of relatively low economic growth, GDP growth went up to 5.2 per cent in 1974–1979 and to 5.5 per cent in the 1980s. The inflation rate came down sharply from the 'hyper-inflationary' early 1970s, and agricultural production was also buoyant. The one major cause for concern remained the external economic situation, particularly since oil prices were again under pressure due to disturbed geopolitical conditions in West Asia. The Cold War arrived close to India with the Soviet invasion of Afghanistan and the US decision to respond to it.

Returning to office as the prime minister, Indira Gandhi issued a new SIP in 1980 with a focus on promoting exports so that the pressure on balance of payments caused by the oil crisis could be eased. India sought a loan from the IMF to tide over the pressure on the balance of payments caused by the sharp rise in the oil import bill. Inward remittances of foreign exchange from an increasing number of Indian workers in the Gulf region helped partly mitigate the stress on the current account. The 1980 SIP specified eight objectives:

1. optimum utilization of existing industrial capacity;
2. maximizing productivity and production;
3. higher employment generation;
4. correction of regional imbalances through preferential development of backward areas;
5. promotion of agro-based industries;
6. promotion of export-oriented industries;
7. promotion of economic federalism through dispersed industrialization and promotion of small-scale industries; and
8. assurance and fair prices and good quality in consumer interest.

The new policy also liberalized the regulation of monopolies and foreign exchange utilization and placed greater emphasis on the growth of private enterprise. A further acceleration of industrial and trade policy liberalization occurred after Rajiv Gandhi took over as prime minister in 1984. The government also began focusing on promoting new technologies, especially electronics, and new industries, including telecommunications and information technology. A gradual easing of licencing policy began with several industries like two-wheelers, pharmaceuticals, petrochemicals and paper exempted from certain licencing provisions.

MSME POLICY

An important component of industrial policy through the plan period has been the support extended to small-scale industries. A legacy of Gandhian thinking on economics was the protection extended to khadi and village industries that has endured over the years. Apart from this, the government extended policy support to the modern small-scale sector, more recently referred to as 'micro, small and medium enterprises' (MSME), to encourage the growth of new enterprise, facilitate dispersed industrial development and reduce the concentration of economic power.

For the purpose of policy, MSMEs have had several classifications. In the past, the classification was based on the number of workers employed. So, the smallest enterprise unit would be one worker wherein the owner and worker are the same person, such as a roadside cobbler; microenterprises would have up to nine workers; small enterprises would employ between 10 and 49; medium-sized ones would hire 50 to 249 workers and all enterprises with 250 or more workers would be classified as large enterprises. More recently, the Union Government has reclassified MSMEs on the basis of investment and turnover. Thus firms with up to ₹1 crore investment and less than ₹5 crores turnover are classified as microenterprises; firms with an investment of up to ₹10 crores and turnover of less than ₹50 crores are classified as small enterprises; and firms with up to ₹50 crores investment and less than ₹250 crores turnover as medium enterprises.[3]

The manufacture of certain goods like toys, sports goods, furniture, and so on have been reserved for the small-scale sector, with the list changing from time to time. The public sector encouraged MSMEs by subcontracting works and promoting ancillaries. The definition of what constitutes a small-scale firm has changed over time. Moreover, the MSME sector has also got differentiated between more capital-intensive and less capital-intensive firms. Previously, the MSME sector was thought to generate more employment than the large-scale sector, however MSMEs in many industries have become even more capital-intensive than large-scale firms. The policy of state governments to extend subsidies to industries located in backward districts has also facilitated the geographical spread of industrialization.

DEVELOPMENTS IN TECHNOLOGY

A significant gap in industrial development policy was the lack of focus on indigenous technology development. Attention was paid initially to domestic research and development (R&D) in certain critical and strategic sectors, including nuclear technology, and subsequently to domestic R&D in biotechnology, contributing to the growth of the pharmaceuticals industry, there was little investment in R&D by the private sector industry. Nearly all major business houses depended on imported technology in almost all major sectors through the twentieth century. Economist Deepak Nayyar has observed, 'Market structures and government policies have not combined to provide an environment which would accelerate the absorption of imported technology and foster the development of indigenous technology, or create a milieu conducive to diffusion and innovation.'[4] Perhaps this gap in technological development was also because the best engineers produced by the best institutions of technology opted to become managers and marketing professionals rather than enter the industrial shop floor and become engaged in production.

The exceptions to this rule, of the neglect of domestic R&D apart from space and nuclear industries, were pharmaceuticals and information technology. Rajiv Gandhi also encouraged indigenous development of communications technology even though it did not make the same progress in subsequent years as it did in China, which has emerged as a leader in this sector. The fact that while India is a major exporter of software services, it remains an importer of electronic hardware is testimony to the neglect of industrial development of technology. As a consequence, technology imports remain a major component of total imports and electronic hardware technology imports are among the top imports in recent years.

The link between trade and industrialization remains strong given this import dependence in technology. The Make in India programme and the Atmanirbhar Bharat Abhiyan, and the Production Linked Incentives (PLI) scheme are aimed at promoting localization of manufacturing and development of indigenous technologies. We shall return to a discussion of this in a subsequent chapter.

A major gap in industrial development has been the inadequate absorption of the workforce, especially in large-scale manufacturing. While there was some expansion of factory employment in the 1950s, the rate of growth of employment generation in large-scale industry began to decelerate after the mid-60s. Most Five-Year Plans, in any case, focused on national income growth without a specific focus on employment generation. It was only in the short-lived Eighth Five-Year Plan, during the tenures of prime ministers V.P. Singh and Chandra Shekhar Singh, that employment generation became the focus of the Plan. To quote industrial economist J.C. Sandesara, 'The "central thrust" (of Approach Paper of 8th Five-Year Plan, 1990) is employment, whereas in the earlier plans it was GDP. This thrust arises out of the fact that in the election manifesto of the National Front, the "right to work" is a major promise.'[5]

The organized sector in the industrial economy has never been a major source of employment, with the non-industrial sectors continuing to absorb a greater share of workforce. The manufacturing sector, which has accounted for 16 per cent of the GDP, employs only 12 per cent of the total workforce. The data for the year 2020 shows that the agricultural sector absorbed 40 per cent of the workforce while the manufacturing, real estate and construction, and mining sectors absorbed 21 per cent of total employment. This suggests that over the past five years, employment opportunities in the urban economy have shrunk, forcing rural labour to remain at home.

The Union Government has responded to a slowdown in industrial development, accompanied by rising trade deficits, by raising tariffs. Customs duties have been increased on a range of products over the past five Union Budgets. While the objective of trade and industrial policy has been to make domestic industry globally competitive and promote self-reliance, the inability of domestic manufacturing to provide employment remains a key challenge for policy. We will return to a discussion of the Make in India programme in Chapter 12.

STATE AND CRONY CAPITALISM

The term 'crony capitalism' has become commonplace these days. It refers to a nexus between persons in power in government—politicians, officials and regulators—and business persons. Both seek favours from each other. In a regulated and bureaucratic system, business persons seek permits and licences and escape from conviction if caught with wrongdoing of one kind or another, while politicians seek funds on both party political and personal accounts. The phenomenon is universal, only the scale and its consequences for the economy vary.

The fraternal relationship between politicians and business persons dates back to the national movement when politicians seeking India's freedom were often financially supported by the nascent Indian nationalist capitalists. Several eminent business leaders like G.D. Birla, Walchand Hirachand and Lala Shriram were known to be benefactors of the INC. To return the favour extended by them, the Congress party ministers in provincial governments would extend support where and when needed to such benefactors. This relationship continued through the era of 'socialistic' policy in the 1950s, even when most business persons were unhappy with Nehru's policies. The business community was divided on whether or not to support the newly formed Swatantra Party that opposed Nehru's turn to the ideological left, his concept of building a 'socialistic pattern of society' and the licence-permit-quota-raj that accompanied it.[6]

Created by some disillusioned and liberal Congressmen,

led by C. Rajagopalachari, Minoo Masani and N.G. Ranga, the Swatantra Party, rejected Nehru's socialism and the licence-permit-quota raj and sought a more open and liberal market economy. It counted among its supporters the business leader J.R.D. Tata, who happily funded the party even as he maintained close personal relations with Nehru. On the other hand, the other senior business leader, G.D. Birla, rejected the Swatantra Party saying its politics were not 'businessman's politics', and continued to support the Congress party. Not surprisingly, the Birla family ended up cornering the largest number of industrial licences. Not only did the Birlas corner the largest number of licences, but they also pre-empted rivals by sitting on many licences and not implementing them.[7] The Industrial Licensing Policy Inquiry Committee (ILPIC), in its 1967 report, noted such misuse of the licencing system but only recommended changes to it rather than suggesting wholesale scrapping of the system.[8]

Even the appointment of ILPIC was on account of the mounting criticism of the licencing system on the grounds that it had, in fact, favoured large industrial houses and had contributed to the emergence of monopolistic and oligopolistic practices by these large houses. It drew attention to collusion between government and business. Fifteen years after Independence, this unhealthy nexus between government and business in the name of licencing and regulation was alluded to in the Santhanam Committee Report on Prevention of Corruption (1962).[9] It pointed in particular to the practice of several senior government officials taking up assignments in the corporate sector immediately after retirement. The committee suggested a reasonable 'cooling off' period so as to reduce the chances of a quid pro quo in such appointments.

Apart from such corruption, what began attracting public attention was the fact that despite a government-operated licencing system and the political objective of establishing a 'socialistic pattern of society', the country was experiencing a growing concentration of the fruits of development and growth. In particular, the government was concerned about restrictive trade practices of corporates that seemed to be acquiring monopolistic and oligopolistic powers. An MIC, appointed in 1964 and headed by Justice Kulada Charan (K.C.) Das Gupta, was asked to examine the extent and effect of concentration of economic power in private hands, the prevalence of monopolistic and restrictive trade practices and the legislation required to deal with it. One consequence of the MIC study was that the licencing system was liberalized to an extent, though not done away with. More importantly, the government accepted the report's suggestion to constitute a Monopolies and Restrictive Trade Practices Commission (MRTPC) and passed the MRTP Act in 1969 to this end.

Around the same time, several studies were also published on the growing concentration of economic power and the manner in which large business houses had, in fact, benefitted from the licencing system. One such study by economist R.K. Hazari, commissioned by the Planning Commission and published in 1967, pointed to how certain business houses had benefitted more than others from the licencing system. The report did not recommend doing away with licencing, and, in fact, outlined the rationale for it but did point to how the system in practice favoured large industrial houses. It was perhaps neither a coincidence nor evidence of the entrepreneurship of traditional business houses that through the licence-permit-quota raj era the names of the dominant Indian business houses remained the same—Birla, Tata, Singhania, Shriram, Walchand, Goenka, Sahu Jain, Thapar, Dalmia, Modi and the such. This list of names began changing only in the 1980s with the entry of Ambani, Nusli Wadia, the TVS Group, and so on.

The licencing policy served many objectives, but it certainly did not serve the objective of diversifying the ownership base of Indian big business. That began to happen first in the 1980s when the Green Revolution created new pockets of rural prosperity and created new entrepreneurs in states like Punjab, Haryana, Gujarat, Tamil Nadu and Andhra Pradesh and subsequently, after 1991, when economic liberalization and the emergence of new industries and services sectors facilitated the entry of new business groups.

Prime Minister Rajiv Gandhi and his finance minister, V.P. Singh, set the tone for further trade and industrial policy liberalization with a forward-looking annual budget statement in Parliament in February 1985 that sought to redefine the relationship between the public and private sectors, giving the latter a prominent role in industrial development. Lower taxation rates and the appointment of private sector executives to head public sector companies were all policy signals aimed at giving the private corporate sector an important role in national development. It would be no exaggeration to say that Rajiv Gandhi sought to bring about a new perception of private sector business leadership within the political and bureaucratic class as well as in society as a whole.[10]

The Regime Change of 1991

The year 1991 is now widely recognized as the turning point for economic policy in India. The license-permit-quota raj, and the import-substituting and inward-oriented strategy of trade and industrialization that we have discussed in earlier chapters came to an end. A minority government headed by Prime Minister P.V. Narasimha Rao, including Dr Manmohan Singh as the Union Finance Minister and P. Chidambaram as minister of commerce, overturned the post-Independence trade and industrial policy regime. The economic crisis that preceded this regime change, as I have explained in some detail in a book devoted to the events of that landmark year, was a long time in the making.[1]

Two developments on the economic front queered the pitch. First, a deterioration in the balance of payments was reflected in a higher current account deficit (CAD), that is the sum of the deficit in foreign trade and in capital flows as a share of national income. This went from -1.7 per cent of GDP in 1980–1985 to -2.9 per cent in 1985–1990. Total external debt trebled from $20.6 billion in 1980–1981 to $64.4 billion in 1989–1990, with the share of external debt in national income going up from 17.7 per cent to 24.5 per cent during that period. In all this, the share of private debt kept rising as the government liberalized external commercial borrowing and allowed Indian companies to borrow abroad. The key factor contributing to the sharp rise in CAD in the 1980s was a steep increase in imports—especially defence imports—and in external commercial borrowings of the private sector. After hovering around 3 per cent, the share of defence spending in national income went up to 3.6 per cent in 1986–1987 and 1987–1988.

The second development was a sustained rise in the budget and fiscal deficits. The share of fiscal deficit, defined as the deficit in the government budget and the government's interest payment obligations, in national income shot up from an average of 6.3 per cent in the Sixth Plan period of 1980–1985 to 8.2 per cent in the Seventh Plan period of 1985–1990. Most economists regard this as too high and prefer the number to be below 3 per cent. To make matters worse, the government's internal debt also went up from 36 per cent of the GDP at the end of 1980–1981 to 54 per cent of the GDP at the end of 1990–1991. Interest payments by the government doubled during this decade, with their share in the GDP going up from an annual average of 2.6 per cent in 1980–1985 to 3.9 per cent in 1985–1990.

Even with an overwhelming majority in Parliament, with over 400 MPs on the treasury benches in a house of 542 members, Rajiv Gandhi was unable to steer the economy away from fiscal mismanagement and crisis. Summing up their sharp indictment of the macroeconomic policies of the Rajiv Gandhi government, economists Joshi and Little concluded:

The major mistake of macroeconomic policy lay in neglecting the danger signs evident in 1985–86 on the fiscal front. Fiscal deterioration was allowed to proceed apace. As a consequence, the current account deficit continued to worsen and domestic and foreign debt continued to increase at a dangerous rate. By the end of the decade, the macroeconomic fundamentals were out of joint. Even a strictly temporary shock like the Gulf War was enough to trigger a full-scale crisis.[2]

The eminent economist Dr I.G. Patel, governor of the RBI from 1977 to 1982, termed the deterioration in the economic situation as 'the greatest crisis we have faced since Independence.' He accused 'successive governments in the 1980s' of 'abdicating their responsibility to the nation for the sake of short-term partisan political gains and indeed out of sheer political cynicism.'[3]

The deterioration in the economic situation resulted in Moody's, the New York-headquartered credit rating agency, undertaking an assessment of the India risk, that is, the risk of lending to the Indian government and to entities whose debt is guaranteed by the government. It looked at the fiscal implications of the V.P. Singh government's decision to write off a part of the loan given by banks to farmers; the fiscal and economic impact of extending reservations and the likelihood of a minority government taking adequate policy action to deal with growing external and domestic fiscal pressures.

In placing India on 'credit watch for possible downgrading' on 1 August 1990, it was not just a weakening of India's economic indicators that Moody's worried about. In its risk assessment report, Moody's drew attention to increasing communal friction, continued tension in the Punjab, Kashmir and the northeastern region, and the situation in Tamil Nadu, and concluded: 'Political conditions in India have weakened since our initial rating assignment (in 1987).'[4]

Moody's decided to place India's ratings on review for a possible downgrade because it feared an increase in two kinds of risks.

> First, the risk of a short-term liquidity crunch leaving India unable to finance its external imbalance and forcing her to undertake sharp balance of payments adjustment largely dependent on compressing domestic growth; Second, the risk that measures selected to achieve balance of payments adjustment in the short-term would disrupt the process of structural change, jeopardizing political support for efforts to improve India's international competitive position, in the medium term.[5]

Moody's returned in October 1990 to take another look at India and concluded that things had become worse. The rising external debt burden and falling foreign exchange reserves were major worries. Rising fiscal deficit and decelerating government revenues were the secondary issues. The Gulf crisis had raised fresh concerns about India's capacity to pay for its imports. Reviewing the economic, social and political situation in India, Moody's concluded, 'the government does not have the capacity to achieve a rapid improvement in the government budget deficit [...]and, India's fractious domestic political conditions make it difficult to cut spending that sustains the government's political support.'[6]

When the Chandra Shekhar Singh government was

formed in November 1990, it was familiar with the declining economic situation. But India's political leaders had to come to terms with the fact that it was not just India's 'economic risk' that had gone up, but so had its 'political risk' because a minority government was in office. This was a new problem for India's economic managers. Independent India had faced a balance of payments crises before and had dealt with a variety of other economic difficulties and crises in the half-century of its existence. However, during each such episode, a government with a clear mandate and parliamentary majority had been in office. For the first time, in 1991, a minority government, bereft of any mandate was been charged with the responsibility of dealing with an external payments crisis.

For the first time, 'political risk' appeared on the radar of the rating managers monitoring India risk. On 7 March 1991, Standard & Poor's, who had, thus far, been a step behind Moody's, downgraded India's sovereign rating to BBB minus for long-term credit risk and to A3 for short-term credit risk, based on the conclusion that 'adverse economic conditions or changing circumstances are more likely to lead to a weakened capacity of the obligor to meet its financial commitments'. The 'obligor' in question was the government of the Republic of India.

Against this background, the Chandra Shekhar Singh government decided to approach the IMF for the balance of payments support. An IMF loan would have boosted international confidence in the government's ability to deal with a tough economic situation. The negotiations with IMF, undertaken secretly in December 1990, yielded immediate support of $1.8 billion, made available in January 1991 through a standby arrangement and the IMF's compensatory and contingency financing facility (CCFF).[7] The latter was in part meant to offer a balance of payments support to countries experiencing shortfalls in export earnings due to temporary and unforeseen factors beyond the control of member governments. India qualified for CCFF support since it was hit by a spike in oil prices caused by Iraq's invasion of Kuwait.

While extending a helping hand, the IMF drew attention to India's long-term problems. The mounting external debt situation had been made worse by the fact that the share of short-term debt had risen steeply in recent years. If India wished to avert a payment default, it would be better advised to enter into a medium-term structural adjustment and stabilization programme. The IMF, however, wanted the Indian government to first get its annual budget approved by Parliament, testing its political support as a precondition for a medium-term programme.

The inability of the government to secure parliamentary approval for a regular budget once Rajiv Gandhi withdrew support from the Chandra Shekhar Singh government, resulted in a further downgrading of India's credit rating. The problem was no longer one of numbers—fiscal deficit, external debt and such. What was till then an economic crisis, made worse by the Gulf War and the spike in oil prices, became a crisis of confidence. India's ability to manage a crisis was now in doubt. As the Ranjit Sau summed up the finance ministry's *Economic Survey of 1991–1992*: 'The payments crisis of 1990–91 was not, we are told, due simply to a deterioration in the trade account; it was accompanied by other adverse developments on the capital account reflecting the loss of confidence in the government's ability to manage the economy.'[8]

◆

On the evening of 22 June, a day after being sworn into office, Prime Minister P.V. Narasimha Rao addressed the nation on television:

> The economy is in a crisis. The balance of payments situation is exceedingly difficult. Inflationary pressures on the price level are considerable. There is no time to lose. The government and the country cannot keep living beyond their means and there are no soft options left. We must tighten our belts and be prepared to make the necessary sacrifices to preserve our economic independence which is an integral part of our vision for a strong nation.[9]

The Prime Minister then took an interesting step forward. Not restricting himself to crisis management, fiscal and balance of payments stabilization, he chose to commit his government to wider economic reform. 'The government is committed to removing the cobwebs that come in the way of rapid industrialization. We will work towards making India internationally competitive, taking full advantage of modern science and technology and opportunities offered by the evolving global economy.'[10]

In two simple sentences, Rao declared to the nation his decision to utilize the crisis as an opportunity to shift India's trade and industrial policy from the inward orientation of the Nehru–Indira years onto a new trajectory of globally integrated development.

The 'evolving global economy' was being reshaped by new geopolitical factors—the disintegration of the Soviet Union and the restructuring of the world trading system by an assertive US. It was the US that had helped create the General Agreement on Trade and Tariffs (GATT) in the 1950s. The purpose of GATT was to install a global trading regime that would enable the war-torn economies of Europe and Asia to rebuild themselves while creating new markets for US exports. The US believed GATT had served its purpose, helping Germany, Japan and many 'East Asian Tigers' emerge as globally competitive economies. Their exports were now threatening the US. The sole superpower wanted to restructure the global trading system, replacing GATT with a new world trade organization.

In India, opinion was already divided among policymakers between those who sought to tackle the balance of payments crisis through 'import-compression' and those who felt the crisis was an opportunity to open up the economy and seek export-oriented investment that would increase India's export earnings. On his very first day as prime minister, Rao told the nation that he would like to see India take advantage of the evolving global economy rather than shut its doors tighter.

While the immediate demands of crisis management, especially the urgent need to avoid default on external debt repayments, required 'import compression', in months to come, Rao lent his weight to trade liberalization and the reintegration of the Indian economy with the global, especially the dynamic East Asian, economies.

◆

The government's immediate task was to avoid default. It was not just the ignominy associated with a default that India wished to avoid. The loss of confidence in a country's ability to manage its economy prudently is not easily reversed. Rao's predecessor had already taken the decision that India would rather mortgage gold than default on external payments. Prime Minister Rao authorized a second round of gold mortgages. The first tranche, undertaken in May 1991, involved the shipment of 20 tonnes of gold. The second round, undertaken in July 1991, involved the movement of around 46.91 tonnes of gold, valued at $400 million, from the RBI vaults in Mumbai to the vaults of the Bank of England in London.[11]

Even as dollars were earned by mortgaging gold, they were lost as non-resident Indians withdrew the cash deposited in foreign currency accounts in India and, in a flight to safety, transferred the funds to banks abroad. Given that the priority for the government was to avert external default, there was no other option but to tighten import controls further. The import squeeze began to hurt the economy, which, on the one hand, slowed down and, on the other, experienced inflationary pressure on the price level. The economy was in the throes of what economists define as stagflation.

Opinion was divided within the government on whether 'import-compression' ought to be ensured through physical controls, an outright ban, or ensured through price signals and devaluation of the rupee. Finance Minister Dr Manmohan Singh tilted in favour of using the exchange rate rather than import bans. Over the financial year 1990–1991, the rupee had already depreciated by around 11 per cent, but it was now felt that a one-time sharp adjustment would stabilize the rupee by renewing confidence in it. On 1 July, the rupee was devalued by around 9 per cent and on 3 July there was a further devaluation by around 11 per cent, with the adjustment working out to a 17.38 per cent devaluation. The rupee slipped from ₹17.90 to a US dollar to ₹24.5. By the end of 1992, it was around ₹31 to a dollar, and remained around that level till the end of Rao's term.

The entire exercise was dubbed 'hop, skip and jump' by Dr Singh and Dr C. Rangarajan, the governor of RBI from 1992 to 1997.[12] It was a game the two played in secrecy. While Singh had secured the Prime Minister's authorization, Rao developed cold feet after the first step, on 1 July 1991. Devaluation was a bad word in Indian politics. Rao would have known of the 1966 devaluation episode and how Indira Gandhi had been criticized for it. Not many are aware of the fact that when Indira Gandhi devalued the rupee in 1966, again under the IMF's advice, she took care to depute officials from the PMO and finance ministry to several state capitals so that important chief ministers were briefed about it. A sudden change in the value of the rupee had to be politically managed. It was not just an economic decision.

Once the two-step action was taken, government spokespersons moved in fast to assure the markets that there would be no further devaluation. The rupee had found its warranted level. The markets stabilized.

Following the devaluation, the government began the process of liberalizing the trade regime, moving away from India's traditional export pessimism to a new philosophy that viewed exports as another source of growth as well as a source of foreign exchange. India is a resources-deficient economy in per capita terms and was vitally dependent on oil imports. It needed to finance not just essential imports but also export-promoting imports in sectors using new technologies.

No sooner had the devaluation exercise been completed

than Rao moved on the trade policy front, authorizing an end to the standard operating procedure given to exporters called the Cash Compensatory System (CCS). This was a subsidy given to exporters to compensate for all the inefficiencies of the Indian system that made exports globally uncompetitive. Devaluation was an incentive for exporters. Hence, on the same day that the RBI took the second step on rupee devaluation, CCS was withdrawn, ignoring apprehensions of the commerce ministry, which has long regarded its dharma to be the defence of the interests of exporters.

On 3 July, as directed by the Prime Minister, Finance Minister Singh called in Commerce Minister Chidambaram and the Commerce Secretary Montek Singh Ahluwalia and instructed them to prepare papers abolishing CCS and get the Prime Minister's signature. Singh told them that with the rupee devalued, the government could afford to displease exporters by withdrawing this subsidy. The politician in Chidambaram balked at the idea. Dr Singh had to tell the commerce minister then that the Prime Minister wanted the orders issued the same day. By the end of the day, CCS was abolished.

Two key considerations defined trade policy reform: first, to enable India to move closer to the emerging new global trade policy architecture that was to be put in place by the yet-to-be-established World Trade Organization (WTO); second, to link import entitlements to export performance. The bureaucratic system of the government granting import licenses was replaced by a market mechanism that would enable exporters to earn 'exim scrips' that could be traded on the market, and importers would be able to buy the scrips to pay for their imports. This was a transitional arrangement that sought to ensure trade balance.

Combining devaluation with trade policy liberalization made sense. These measures also aimed to demonstrate to international investors and financial institutions that the new minority government was prepared to make difficult decisions. Thus the efforts were aimed as much at boosting confidence in India as they were at securing access to hard currency.

A week after the devaluation exercise and on the eve of the first session of Parliament, Prime Minister Rao addressed the nation for a second time. He explained to the people the logic behind his early policy moves in simple terms. You cannot import if you do not export. 'My motto is trade, not aid. Aid is a crutch. Trade builds pride. India has been trading for thousands of years.'[13] He then went on to emphasize that he intended to go beyond crisis management to bring India in line with the rest of the world.

> We believe that India has much to learn from what is happening elsewhere in the world. Many countries are bringing in far-reaching changes. We find major economic transformation sweeping large countries like [the] Soviet Union and China[...] There is a change in outlook, a change in mindset everywhere. India too cannot lag behind if she has to survive, as she must, in the new environment.

Within a fortnight of taking charge as prime minister, and even before the first sitting of Parliament, Rao took momentous decisions that helped restore confidence in the economy. The next major step to take, and the one that the IMF and the rating agencies were eagerly looking forward to, was a sharp reduction in the fiscal deficit. If exchange rate management was the RBI's job, fiscal management was the finance minister's.

In fact, the most important announcement made in Dr Singh's first Budget speech, on 24 July 1991, was the reduction in the budget deficit. It was a commitment that Yashwant Sinha had first made in December 1990. It was now Dr Manmohan Singh's turn to deliver on that commitment. The fiscal deficit was brought down sharply from a high of 8.4 per cent of the GDP in 1990–1991 to 5.9 per cent in 1991–1992. The Seventh Five-Year Plan average was as high as 8.2 per cent. This was, by any standard, a sharp and decisive cut.

Reducing the fiscal deficit by two percentage points of the GDP meant squeezing government expenditure sharply. In the long run, a government's deficit can also be reduced by raising revenues. But the crisis and the IMF's conditions for extending balance of payments support required a surgical cut in the expenditure in one go. Dr Singh was candid in his budget speech in Parliament, 'The crisis of the fiscal system is a cause for serious concern. [...] Without decisive action now, the situation will move beyond the possibility of corrective action.'[14] He proposed a steep reduction in subsidies—food, fertilizer and exports—and reduced spending on defence aimed at bringing the fiscal deficit down.

Dr Manmohan Singh's budget speech has become a landmark policy statement. His detailed explanation of the origins of the balance of payments and fiscal crisis, his defence of government response and his proposals for reform were spelt out clearly in his usual, soft-spoken manner. The Lok Sabha heard him in silence. The press and visitors' galleries were full. The nation watched him on television as he summed up his long 31-page speech of over 18,000 words with the dire warning that a 'grave economic crisis' faced the country but that the government would take 'determined action'.

The last paragraph of that historic Budget speech has since been etched on the minds of successive generations of economic policymakers:

> Sir, I do not minimise the difficulties that lie ahead on the long and arduous journey on which we have embarked. But as Victor Hugo once said, 'no power on earth can stop an idea whose time has come'. I suggest to this august House that the emergence of India as a major economic power in the world happens to be one such idea. Let the whole world hear it loud and clear. India is now wide awake. We shall prevail. We shall overcome.[15]

Exchange rate adjustment and fiscal deficit reduction would have been enough to win the confidence of credit rating agencies and financial markets. However, Rao went a step beyond. Intervening in the debate on the motion of thanks to the President for his address to Parliament, on 15 July, Rao claimed, 'All [our] measures were really written about in newspapers times without number[...] So it is not as if the measures which we have taken have just dropped from the heaven overnight[...] People are more knowledgeable than myself on what is happening in the Soviet Union [...] we cannot keep out of this change, this complete global sweeping change that is coming.'[16]

On 24 July, Prime Minister Rao, in his capacity as the Union Minister for Industries, authorized his junior minister, P.J. Kurien, to make public his new industrial policy statement, dismantling the license-permit-quota raj. The early emergency measures of July were followed up by more sustained efforts at economic liberalization, industrial policy reform and fiscal stabilization in the months to come. In September, the government issued an ordinance removing restrictions on capacity expansion, mergers, acquisitions, amalgamation and takeovers that had been closely controlled until then by the MRTP Act of 1969.

By November, the Finance Minister was able to seal a deal with the World Bank for financing under its enhanced structural adjustment facility (ESAF) and with the IMF for a standby loan of $2.2 billion. As foreign exchange reserves kept rising, some of the more draconian import curbs were eased, and procedures for foreign investment eased.

Rao's real contribution to economic reform and liberalization was his political management of a contentious process. While Dr Singh provided professional leadership to reforms, Rao provided political backing. Economic liberalization did more than merely step up the rate of growth of the economy. It made it easier for new business groups across the country to grow. As we have already discussed, the license-permit-quota raj had, in fact, facilitated the growth of oligopolies and crony capitalists. Delicencing made it easier for new business groups, especially those based in new centres of industrial activity like Gujarat, Karnataka, Andhra Pradesh and Punjab-Haryana. The regional dispersal of business activity was an important motivator and consequence of economic liberalization. Apart from the 'children of reform', as Dr Manmohan Singh once called them, like Narayana Murthy and Azim Premji of the information technology services business, new business leaders like Anji Reddy in Andhra Pradesh, Baba Kalyani and Habil Khorakiwala in Maharashtra and Sunil Mittal in Delhi, entered the ranks of India's billionaires at the turn of the century.

While the liberalization of industrial policy contributed to the emergence of new enterprises, the liberalization of trade policy enabled India to create new relations of interdependence with the rest of the world. Over the decade 1991–2001, the share of trade in national income increased, and so did India's share of world trade. Interestingly, there was a regional shift in the pattern of trade with India's trade with the wider Asian region, including West Asia, Southeast Asia and South Asia, rising faster than its trade with the US and Europe. China rapidly emerged as a major trade partner, and so did countries like the United Arab Emirates. Prime Minister Narasimha Rao's 'Look East Policy' had a tangible impact on India's trade and investment links with the world.

Expectations shape outcomes in a world of uncertainty. Expectations about the economy end up being self-fulfilling prophecies. If you expect tomorrow to be better than today, you take economic decisions that ensure tomorrow is indeed better. On the other hand, if one believes the future to be bleaker than the present, one ends up making decisions and choices that contribute to a less-than-satisfactory outcome. The policy changes of 1991 altered the 'state of expectations', so to speak, about where India was headed, triggering positive expectations about future growth and stimulating private investment. All successive governments comprising different political parties walked the path set by the initiatives taken in 1991.

Making in India

I n the initial years of trade and industrial policy liberalization, after 1991, higher economic growth translated into a higher share of trade and industrial output in national income. The share of manufacturing sector output in the GDP went up from 15.68 per cent in 1991 to 17.87 per cent in 1995, remaining around 16–17 per cent over the next decade.[1] Even more impressive was the rapid increase in the share of foreign trade in national income. The total trade (exports plus imports) in goods and services went up as a share of GDP from 17 per cent in 1990 to 48.4 per cent in 2007, the year before the transatlantic financial crisis of 2008. By 2014 it exceeded 50 per cent of national income. This impressive rise in the share of foreign trade drew attention to the growing competitiveness of Indian manufacturing and services because it happened against the backdrop of a sharp reduction in average tariffs. The unweighted average applied tariff on manufacturing in 1990 was as high as 145 per cent and this was brought down to 14 per cent by 2005.

Encouraged by this trend, India entered into several bilateral and regional preferential trade agreements (PTAs).

India offered unilateral trade concessions to less developed economies in its neighbourhood and actively engaged East and Southeast Asian economies. India joined the multilateral trading system in 1948 as a founder-member of the GATT. The first regional trade agreement of which India became a member was the Bangkok Agreement in 1975. In December 1998, India signed its first bilateral free trade agreement (FTA) with Sri Lanka, officially called the India-Sri Lanka Free Trade Agreement (ISFTA), and which came into force in 2001. Subsequently, India implemented the South Asian Free Trade Agreement (SAFTA) in 2004, the Comprehensive Economic Cooperation Agreement (CECA) with Singapore in 2005, the ASEAN-India Free Trade Agreement (AIFTA) in 2010, the India-Korea Comprehensive Economic Partnership Agreement (CEPA) in 2010, the India-Malaysia Comprehensive Economic Cooperation Agreement (CECA) and the India-Japan Comprehensive Economic Partnership Agreement (CEPA) in 2011. Though, what remains fairly ambiguous is the impact of these trade agreements on India's export trade. Critics have pointed out that after the conclusion of a free or preferential trade agreement India has found exports to the concerned market not growing as fast as imports from there.

Even within her neighbourhood, India's share of trade has remained low. To facilitate India's trade with her neighbours, the SAARC Preferential Trading Arrangement (SAPTA) was signed in 1993, followed by SAFTA almost a decade later in 2004 (which came into force in 2006). SAFTA has been hobbled by political tensions between India and Pakistan, its two largest members. In 2014, the Narendra Modi government called for a review of all FTAs and PTAs and stopped all further negotiations. However, with the trade-to-GDP ratio dropping sharply after 2015, going down well below 40 per cent by 2020[2], the government opted for a fresh look at trade policy and has renewed trade negotiations with several countries, concluding an FTA with the United Arab Emirates in February 2022.

The main concern shaping trade policy remains the low share of manufacturing in the GDP, stuck at around 17 per cent. Despite the Green Revolution and agrarian prosperity in some parts of the country, the overall size of the home market for manufactured goods remained limited. Slow growth of domestic demand, foodgrains price inflation, deficient supply of raw materials for industries and the policy constraints imposed by a bureaucratic State contributed to major industrial growth stagnation till the 1980s. India's initial unwillingness and the subsequent slow probing of the global market meant that the export-based industrialization of East Asia did not take root in the country. The change in the domestic policy regime after 1991 did help but by the turn of the century, it was evident that industrial growth was not picking up. Critics of trade liberalization blamed this on import competition. For the manufacturing sector, the simple average tariff had fallen from 126 per cent in 1990–1991 to 36 per cent in 1997–1998 and then to 12.1 per cent in 2014–2015.[3]

It was against this background that Prime Minister Dr Manmohan Singh set up the National Manufacturing Competitiveness Council (NMCC) in 2005. In its 2006 report, the Council advocated a new manufacturing strategy. These ideas found their way into what the Planning Commission called *The Manufacturing Plan: Strategies for Accelerating Growth of Manufacturing in India in the 12th Five Year Plan and Beyond.*[4] The document called for a 'paradigm shift' in industrial policy and suggested various policy measures aimed at increasing the share of the manufacturing sector in the GDP from 17 per cent to 25 per cent by 2022. The strategy outlined in this document was subsequently relaunched by Prime Minister Narendra Modi as the Make in India programme.[5]

The Twelfth Five-Year Plan recognized the challenge of 'jobless growth' in the industrial sector and suggested that the 'architecture of industrial policy' needed to change to boost growth. Instead of a hands-off approach of the reform era, India would need to learn and adopt the approach of post-war success stories (Japan, South Korea, China) in growing competitiveness and scale of their manufacturing: close coordination between producers and government policymakers, with governments playing an active role in providing incentives for domestic industrial growth and in relieving constraints on industrial competitiveness.

The National Manufacturing Policy, mooted in 2011, sought to increase 'depth' in manufacturing, enhance the global competitiveness of Indian manufacturing through appropriate policy support and ensure the sustainability of growth, particularly regarding the environment. Achieving a greater depth in manufacturing entails ensuring a higher level of value addition within the country. This requires focus on a few key areas like the heavily import-skewed capital goods sector, technological advancements in nearly all manufacturing sectors and a focus on improved domestic research and development. All this marked a significant change in India's approach to industry/manufacturing in the 'era of planning' that continues today under the new rubric of 'Atmanirbhar Bharat'. The Make in India programme, launched on 25 September 2014, was nothing but a revised version of the National Manufacturing Policy, 2011, of the Manmohan Singh government.

The symbolic lion, signifying the strength of Indian industries, made out of cogwheels, was launched as the power mascot of the Make in India campaign. With India inviting countries to 'Come, Make in India', the programme was anticipated to change the face of the manufacturing sector. To impart to the campaign a trade-promoting angle, the Prime Minister rephrased the programme as 'Make in India, Make for the World'. A multitude of policies aimed at easing the industrial processes was initiated across subsectors. While the primary idea of Make in India was not new, given our prolonged history of hustle with factory production, it aimed to make India the global hub of production. The entire programme was based on three pillars: increasing the annual growth rate of the manufacturing sector to 12–14 per cent; creating additional 100 million manufacturing jobs; and increase the manufacturing sector's contribution to GDP to 25 per cent by 2022. (The target date was subsequently pushed to 2025).[6]

Through this initiative, foreign manufacturers were invited to set up their production units in the country and not just market them. With a prime focus on 25 sectors to boost manufacturing, the programme was launched amidst a lot of hype and attention. The campaign aims to cover a myriad of objectives, including the facilitation of easy investment, provision of an impetus for innovation, skill development, best in class manufacturing infrastructure and, most importantly, the creation of employment avenues. When the programme was launched in 2014–2015, the condition of the manufacturing sector was in shackles, with a mere, stagnated contribution of 17 per cent to the GDP. The growth impetus through the service sector was also reaching saturation for employment absorption. The time called for stringent actions for the manufacturing sector, thus building up the rationale for Make in India.

The rationale behind the Make in India campaign rests on the need for India to become a manufacturing powerhouse in order to gainfully employ the potential demographic dividend. To accommodate the 300 million people who will join India's workforce between 2010 and 2040, each year 10 million jobs must be created.[7] The decision of many developed market economies to 'decouple' from China—that is reduce their dependence on supply chains linked to China—provided India with an opportunity to seek relocation of foreign firms away from China into India. This process is still in its early stages, with several American and European multinationals opting to first relocate to Southeast Asian countries before looking at the India opportunity.

The policy was well structured, outcome-oriented, and a significant initiative to restart the engine of India's manufacturing wagon; however, as some critics have pointed out, 'the lion has not yet roared'. One of the main objectives of the policy, to increase the share of the manufacturing sector in the GDP to 25 per cent, remains nowhere near being met, with this share, in fact, declining to below 16 per cent in 2020. The Index of Industrial Production (IIP) showed negligible growth of around 3 per cent over six years, 2015–2021, clearly implying a lack of impetus for the growth of manufacturing productivity. While India accounts for nearly 85 per cent of the total foreign direct investment (FDI) inflows in South Asia, the manufacturing sector attracts only a quarter of these inflows, with a bulk going into the services sector. A large part of the foreign investment that India has been able to attract has gone into the services rather than the manufacturing sector. Moreover, there has been very little 'greenfield' investment, with a large part of FDI inflows focused on buying up Indian entities.

The Covid-19 pandemic administered further shocks on manufacturing and services sectors, both the supply and demand side. Heavy retrenchment, contraction in factory outputs and lack of demand hit the already suffering manufacturing sector. In 2018 itself, the Periodic Labour Force Survey (PLFS) of 2017–2018 showed that the unemployment rate had touched a 45-year high at 6.1 per cent.[8] The employment situation in manufacturing became worse after 2020.

Concerned about the slow progress of the Make in India initiative and the inadequate competitiveness of Indian manufacturing at a time when the global trading environment was becoming increasingly protectionist, the government launched a scheme to facilitate focused development of critical industrial sectors. Called the Production Linked Incentives scheme, this new experiment in what economists call 'industrial policy' was launched in March 2020. Initially, the scheme sought to promote mobile and electric components manufacturing, pharmaceuticals (including active pharmaceutical ingredients) and medical devices manufacturing. It was later expanded to include automobiles and auto components, drones and drone components, advanced chemical cell batteries, electronics hardware and information technology hardware, food processing, specialty steel, white goods and solar photovoltaic modules, telecom and networking products, and textiles and apparels.

The focus of the PLI scheme has been on promoting sunrise industries, new technologies as well as labour-intensive manufactures. The government hopes to plug Indian industry into the global value and supply chains through this initiative. It is, therefore, a trade and industrialization policy woven together. The scheme has been conceived such that government-funded financial incentives are provided only after the relevant investment is made, employment has been generated, and production and sales targets are achieved. The PLI scheme has incentives specially targeted at the MSME sector. PLI, it is hoped, would help reduce imports, build domestic manufacturing capacities, and promote exports.

Faced with the problem of slow industrialization and, worse, a decline in the rate of private sector capital formation, the government has been forced to devise strategies to boost investment in industry, especially the manufacturing sector. The share of gross fixed capital formation in the GDP increased from around 24 per cent in the early 1990s to a peak of 36 per cent by 2007–2008 and then began to decline, touching a low of 27 per cent in 2020.[9] Over the past couple of decades, most policy efforts have been aimed at reversing this trend and reviving industrial sector growth. While the competition from China and other export-oriented economies has partly contributed to the problems of domestic industry, there is also a feeling among Indian business that despite the so-called improvement in the 'ease-of-doing business' in India, the domestic environment is still far too challenging for industrial development.

The Make in India programme and the PLI scheme have been policy responses aimed at altering the policy environment. More recently, through the Union Budget statement of February 2022, the government has once again tapped into the earlier, what may be called the 'Nehruvian', strategy of public investment-led growth in the industrial sector. Union Finance Minister Nirmala Sitharaman explained the new policy of seeking to 'crowd-in' private investment by undertaking public investment as follows:

> Capital investment holds the key to speedy and sustained economic revival and consolidation through its multiplier effect. Capital investment also helps in creating employment opportunities, inducing enhanced demand for manufactured inputs from large industries and MSMEs, services from professionals, and help farmers through better agri-infrastructure. [...] [T]he virtuous cycle of investment requires public investment to crowd-in private investment. At this stage, private investments seem to require that support to rise to their potential and to the needs of the economy. Public investment must continue to take the lead and pump-prime the private investment and demand.[10]

In that statement, we hear, once again, the echoes of the Bombay Plan, the Mahalanobis Plan and the 'mixed economy' model of public—private partnership. Once again, the State has intervened to push capitalist industrialization forward. Even as the government stepped in to invest in infrastructure and industry, it privatized Air India and opened up defence manufacturing to private investment. The Finance Minister's Budget speech also claimed that the PLI scheme covering

14 sectors would achieve the vision of Atmanirbhar Bharat, creating 60 lakh new jobs and stepping up production by ₹30 lakh crore during 2022–2027. The Finance Minister also announced an increase in tariffs across several sectors, with a focus on products manufactured by the MSME sector. In that sense, the new industrial policy is not a return to the old industrial policy. However, it is a variant of the same model of State-assisted capitalist development that India has followed since Independence.

13

A Services Economy

A longstanding hypothesis in development economics has been that economic growth and progress entail a decline in the share of the agricultural sector in national income even as the share of the industrial sector rises. Subsequently, at some higher level of industrialization, as the economy becomes more complex with the growth of financial, banking, trading and other services, the service sector would begin to grow. Many old and newly industrializing economies of Europe and East Asia followed this path, thus confirming the validity of this view of development. China, Taiwan, South Korea, Japan and most of the advanced western economies went through this trajectory before attaining prosperity. But not all developing countries have experienced this linear process, nor is the timeline for it very clear. The newly industrializing economies of East Asia did so rapidly, while the process in India has been gradual and halting.

India's economic planners, therefore, quite understandably prioritized industrial development through successive Five-Year Plans. While the initial neglect of agriculture ended in the 1970s, what most economists studying India did not expect was that over time, it would be the services sector that would fuel economic growth, with the industrial sector's share in national income stagnating. Let's look at the numbers. Today, the services sector contributes to over 60 per cent of the GDP, with agriculture accounting for about 15 per cent and the industrial sector totalling up to around 24 per cent. As we have already noted, within the industrial sector, manufacturing alone accounts for no more than 17 per cent, with construction and transport making up for most of the rest. The phenomenal rise in the share of the services sector in the GDP has been partly due to the growth of public spending and partly on account of the growth of a range of new economic activities, such as banking and finance, communications and information technology, and trade and professional services (Table 13.1).

Table 13.1: Sectoral Composition of Gross Domestic Product (Percentage)

Sector	1950s	1960s	1970s	1980s	1990s	2000s	2021
Agriculture	55.4	47.6	42.8	37.4	30.9	21.8	15.4
Industry	14.8	19.6	21.3	22.3	23.3	24.5	23.1
Services	29.8	32.8	35.9	40.3	45.8	53.7	61.5

Source: Economic Survey (Various Years), Ministry of Finance, Government of India.

The services sector includes activities such as wholesale and retail trade, repair of motor vehicles and motorcycles, transportation and storage, hotels, hospitality and food service activities, information and communication, financial and insurance activities, real estate, professional, scientific and technical services, administrative and support services including public administration, defense services, social welfare, education, healthcare, media, arts and entertainment, household services, and so on.

In the first three Five-Year-Plan periods, 1951–1966, sectors like transport, storage, trade, hotels and communications contributed most to the growth of the services sector, apart from government administration and defence. The early years of gradual liberalization in the 1980s saw the growth of banking, finance and business services, while the post-liberalization era of the 1990s and early 2000s saw the phenomenal growth of communication, information technology services, and transport and business services.

A major concern with respect to what many have viewed as unbalanced growth, that is the rapid growth of services sector compared to the stagnation in the share of industrial sector relates to employment generation. There are two aspects to this problem. The first is that of numbers and the second, of the type of employment. The process of development and technological modernization has inevitably led, in most countries, to labour-displacing growth in agriculture. The surplus labour generated by the agrarian sector has then found employment in the urban industrial economy. However, with industrialization being both capital-intensive (and therefore, not adequately labour-absorbing) and dependent on imported capital goods, the industrial sector has not been able to generate as many jobs as required. Both the process of labour displacement from agriculture and population growth have contributed to millions of young people seeking employment in urban and industrial sectors.

A second reason why labour-intensive industrialization has helped the development process is that the manufacturing and construction sectors can absorb low-skilled workers coming out of rural areas and adapting to work in urban areas. While the services sector too provides such employment opportunities at the lower end, as in trade and transportation, most service sector jobs require higher skill and education levels. More recently, the service sector has come to account for about 33 per cent of total employment in the country compared to 26 per cent in industry and 41 per cent in agriculture. These shares, compared with 22, 15 and 63 per cent respectively, in 1990. In other words, the share of agriculture in total employment has sharply reduced, and that of services and industry have increased over the past three decades.

According to a 2010 study by the Asian Development Bank (ADB), a large part of the organized employment in the services sector has been concentrated mainly in the public sector.[1] While the private and household sectors may well employ a bulk of the workforce in services, these would not be in what is defined as the 'organized' sector, that is where the workers have assured wages and codified working conditions, for example in public sector banks and public transport organizations. The working conditions in the private service sector leave much to be desired in terms of security of employment, income and social welfare benefits. To quote the ADB study:

> The service sector will be able to contribute to inclusive growth by enhancing investment, creating employment and human capital, and developing infrastructure. It is

important for a developing country like India with a large, young population to generate quality employment and to move up the value chain.

TRADE IN SERVICES

In the 1980s, as the global trading system transitioned from the GATT to a more rules-based WTO, Indian negotiators resisted the inclusion of trade in services into the multilateral free trade system. However, as the export of services, especially of Indian service providers, boomed through the 1990s, the government changed its views and India actively participated in negotiations for global rules of the game for both the export of services and what is called the 'movement of natural persons', that is the out-migration of workers providing services. Millions of Indians work in a variety of service sector professions around the world. A bulk of them, approximately nine million, are based in the countries of the Gulf Cooperation Council (GCC), while there are at least 80,000 H-1B visa holders in the US.

India earns over $80 billion annually in inward remittances from the GCC region, including Saudi Arabia, Kuwait, UAE, Bahrain, Qatar and Oman. On top of this, India earns over $65 billion from software services exports to developed economies, especially the US. However, there has been a tapering off of inflows partly due to local policies in the region to hire more nationals and fewer immigrants, and partly due to the impact of the Covid-19 pandemic. However, foreign exchange remittances earned through services exports will remain an important element in India's balance of payments management.

Given its competitiveness in services, India has sought preferential access for trade in services and has sought its inclusion along with trade in goods in the various bilateral, plurilateral and regional trade agreements. The WTO also has an agreement for trade in services. The impact of the export trade in services has been substantial on the urban economy. New urban centres near Bengaluru, Gurugram, Hyderabad, Pune and elsewhere have rapidly grown to accommodate service providers in a wide range of businesses, including banking and finance, business data processing, information technology, healthcare management, and so on. Trade in services have increased from $6 billion in 1985 to $205 billion in 2018. Service exports have grown faster than the export of merchandise over the past two decades. While India has always had a deficit on the merchandise trade account, with imports being more than exports, it enjoys a surplus on the services trade account.

Trade in services as a percentage of the GDP increased from 3.2 per cent in 1980 to 13.9 per cent in 2010. While in the 1980s, trade in services contributed to 20 per cent of India's total trade, by 2010s it increased to over 30 per cent compared, much above the global average. Moreover, India's share in world trade in services increased from less than 1 per cent to more than 3 per cent between 1980 and 2010, while its share in merchandise goods trade increased from 0.5 per cent in 1990 to just around 1 per cent in the 2010s.[2] This was one important reason why India sought 'comprehensive economic partnership agreements' rather than a pure FTA or PTA because the latter are focused mainly on trade in goods, while India seeks access to foreign markets in services as well.

The rapid expansion of the services sector at home

and its successful globalization contrasts with the relative stagnation of the industrial sector's share in the GDP and trade. The consequent frustration with industrial growth has encouraged many policymakers and economists to suggest that India may have to consider an altogether different model of development, based on the growth of the services sector as the primary driver of growth and employment generation. The most recent advocate of this line of thinking is Dr Raghuram Rajan, the former governor of the RBI, who has added his voice to the view that India should seek growth by tapping the global trade in services, providing cross border services in a range of sectors.

As much as 70 per cent of the GDP of developed economies is accounted for by services, given the growing importance of business and financial services, trade, healthcare and education. The Covid-19 pandemic has demonstrated the potential of cross-border economic activity without the physical movement of persons, says Rajan.[3] He cites the example of class IV employees at the RBI educating their children to the point where they are able to find employment in this new services economy.[4] So, can this not be the route to social advance and economic development?

There is one problem. What a class IV employee in a public sector organization can afford can certainly not be afforded by a first-generation literate or even semi-literate moving from a rural to an urban environment in search of livelihood security. Traditionally low-skilled manufacturing, especially in small enterprises, provided an entry point, apart from construction work. With even the small and medium enterprises opting increasingly for capital-intensive technologies and not offering adequate employment opportunities for the low and unskilled workers, construction remains the main source of employment. Finally, a large country like India requires a sizeable industrial, scientific and technological base capable of sustaining the growth of critical and strategic industries. This, too, requires a sizeable industrial base. Hence, the view that India can skip the manufacturing stage and depend mainly, if not only, on services sector growth may be a limiting perspective. In this context, we have seen that the government had launched a new industrial policy seeking to 'make in India.'

However, be it manufacturing or services, or even agriculture, it is essential for the Indian economy to be globally competitive in investment in human capabilities. Labour productivity, creativity and enterprise are all a function of societal investment in education, skill development and training. Thus, across all sectors, India needs a more knowledge-based economy. The rise of the services sector and its global competitiveness, compared to agriculture and manufacturing, in fact, underscores the importance of creating domestic human capacity and capability. India cannot remain globally competitive as a services economy merely on the basis of the low cost of human services, be it high skilled or low skilled, white-collar or blue-collar, employee or worker. For the service sector to be an engine of income growth and employment generation, it will have to be manned by a skilled and highly productive workforce capable of providing quality services efficiently and at competitive prices.

The rising overseas migration of young Indians in search of education, especially in disciplines such as medicine, management and finance, suggests that domestic training capacity is inadequate, quantitatively and qualitatively. That foreign investment is being sought for skill development in construction and manufacturing-related services also points to a domestic gap in this regard. Future growth of the services economy will be critically dependent on the quality and availability of education and skill development.

14

Comprehensive National Power

The year 1991 marked a turning point for India, and not just on the economic front. The events of that year also required Indian political leadership to re-examine the relationship between economic performance, capacity and capability, on the one hand, and national power and the capacity to defend one's sovereignty and integrity, on the other. The fiscal and balance of payments crises had not only exerted pressure on the government's fiscal ability to spend on defence and development but also exposed it to external dependence as a consequence of the policy regime thrust upon the country by the IMF and its principal shareholders—the developed economies. It is a different matter that many of the policies adopted, as a consequence, were, in fact, policies that many in India had long advocated and proved to be beneficial for the country's economic growth. However, the fact that the nation had become vulnerable to external pressure alerted the political leadership to the need to take stock of where the country stood and what it needed to do to preserve its sovereignty and integrity.

The fact that the economic crisis India faced was partly

linked to events outside the country left its imprint on the thinking of the national leadership. The war in the Gulf had pushed up oil prices. The decline and implosion of the Soviet Union—India's principal ally through the Cold War era—made matters worse. Many new nations formed in the middle of the twentieth century in Asia and Africa, had not survived their teething years. The countries that joined hands with India to launch the Non-Aligned Movement (NAM)— Egypt, Indonesia, Ghana and Yugoslavia—were all in crisis, with Yugoslavia eventually breaking up owing to political upheavals and strife.

The trigger behind the fiscal and balance of payments crisis of 1990–1991 was twofold. One, a sudden increase in defence spending and defence imports in the second half of the 1980s. The second was the implosion of the Soviet Union under the weight of its economic weaknesses, partly on account of excessive investment in defence and inadequate investment in economic capabilities. Both events shaped new thinking about the relationship between national security and economic performance. Finally, the rise of China through the 1980s and 1990s, based on a more open economic model, mimicking the export-led industrial strategy of much of East Asia, also influenced Indian thinking on economic policy.

China's switch to the Dengist economic model of more outward-oriented industrialization and the emphasis on international trade and the development of comprehensive national power began to change attitudes in India. In his televised national address on 9 July 1991, after his announcement of the first round of trade liberalization, Prime Minister P.V. Narasimha Rao said:

> We believe that India has much to learn from what
> is happening elsewhere in the world. Many countries
> are bringing in far-reaching changes. We find major
> economic transformation sweeping large countries like
> the Soviet Union and China[...] There is a change in
> outlook, a change in mindset everywhere. India too
> cannot lag behind if she has to survive, as she must, in
> the new environment.[1]

The change in thinking on the role of external economic
relations in national development reflected a more
fundamental shift in approach to the idea of 'self-reliance',
national security and global interdependence. Most
postcolonial nations in Asia, Latin America and Africa
viewed external economic relations as imposing a burden
on their developmental aspirations. This thinking defined
the views of the 'Dependency School' in development
economics. Across the developing world, the strategy of
inward orientation was defended on the grounds that it
preserved the independence of newly liberated nations,
reduced dependence on colonial and imperial powers,
and afforded a free economic and political space within
which these new nations could grow. In the social sciences
literature, this spawned such radical schools of thought as
the 'Dependencias', influenced by the work of Raul Prebisch,
Andre Gunder Frank, Immanuel Wallerstein and Samir
Amin. The 'dependency theory' viewed the global economy
as an integrated system in which countries at the 'centre' or
the 'core'—the developed economies, that is the founding
members of the Organisation for Economic Co-operation
and Development (OECD)—derived undue benefit from their

economic interaction with the countries on the 'periphery'—
the developing economies. The underdevelopment of the
latter was intrinsically linked to the development of the
former. It was a zero-sum world.

The new perspective on economic policy shifted the focus
from the idea of 'dependence' to that of 'interdependence',
and insisted that such economic interdependence offered
greater national security. Increasingly, the view held was
that several newly industrializing economies, including large
economies such as China, had been able to increase their
political leverage in international affairs, both in bilateral
relations and in multilateral forums, by increasing their share
of world trade, particularly their trade relationship with the
US and other major OECD economies. Economic relations
acquired a new political dimension in the age of pragmatism
in foreign policy. No country has been able to demonstrate
the power of commerce in diplomacy better than Dengist
China. India followed with a lag.[2] As we have already seen,
the policies adopted since 1991 increased India's share of
world trade and created new 'geo-economic' relationships
with developed economies that eventually shaped India's
geopolitical thinking.

MEASURING NATIONAL POWER

Taken together, these developments influenced thinking at
the highest levels on national security planning. By the end
of the decade, in 1999, the 'Economic Security' chapter of
the *Strategic Defence Review* (SDR) prepared by the National
Security Advisory Board (NSAB) of India would open with
the proposition:

Economic power is the cornerstone of a nation's power in the contemporary world. The economic size of a nation matters and is an important element of national security. Low economic growth, low productivity of capital and labour, inadequate investment in human capital and human capability and a reduced share of world trade have contributed to the marginalization of the Indian economy in the world economy. The economic security challenge for India is to pursue above average national income growth at the annual rate of at least 7 per cent to 8 per cent so that India's share of world income is commensurate with her population size and a larger economic base can more truly reflect India's global status.[3]

This shift in focus away from a narrow view of national security defined by military spending and defence capability to a wider economic perspective was also in step with the new thinking on 'comprehensive national power' (CNP) popularized by the China Academy of Social Sciences (CASS). CASS developed a measure of CNP, defining it as a weighted average of military, economic, scientific and technological capability. The eight variables used were: natural resources (weight of 0.08), domestic economic capability (0.28), external economic capability (0.13), scientific and technological capability (0.15), social development (0.10), military capability (0.10), government capability (0.08) and foreign affairs capability (0.08).[4]

The idea of CNP is as important a contribution to the understanding of a country's overall standing as concepts such as the GDP and the more recently developed concept of human development. GDP was defined by the Nobel Prize-winning economist Simon Kuznets as the sum of all goods and services produced by individuals and firms within a country. Developed in the 1930s, the GDP measure was adopted internationally in 1945 when the IMF and the World Bank used this measure to rank member countries within these multilateral organizations. For half a century, countries were ranked according to their GDP. In the early 1990s, two South Asian economists, Dr Amartya Sen of India (also a Nobel Prize-winning economist) and Dr Mahbub ul Haq of Pakistan, developed a new concept that ranked countries not just by the value of the output and incomes they generated but also by their educational and health status. The new measure was dubbed Human Development Index (HDI). A country like the US may rank high in terms of GDP, but ranks far below a country like Sweden on HDI, because the average Swede has better educational and health attainments than the average American.

In 2020, India had a total GDP of close to $3 trillion and was ranked the sixth-largest economy in the world. However, India was ranked at 131 out of 189 nations in terms of HDI. In other words, while India was generating incomes and output that made it the world's sixth-largest economy, its poor educational and health outcomes had pulled its rank down. Thus, Sen and several other economists have long argued that India should devote more resources to improving its educational and health status.[5]

Into this world of GDP and HDI, Chinese scholars at CASS introduced the idea of CNP, which accounted not just for a country's economic status (in terms of output and income) but also for its human development achievement and, in addition, its scientific, technological, military, diplomatic and governmental capability and capacity. The Chinese CNP indices calculated for the year 1985 showed the US at the top, followed by the Soviet Union; China was seventh and India eleventh (see Table 14.1). The Chinese CNP index had a profound influence on strategic thinking in India and spawned several attempts at constructing similar indices.[6]

Table 14.1: Index of Comprehensive National Power, 1985

Country Rank	Country Name
1	US
2	Soviet Union
3	Japan
4	Germany
5	UK
6	France
7	China
8	Canada
9	Italy
10	Australia
11	India

Source: Singh, P.K., Y.K. Gera and S. Dewan, *Comprehensive National Power: A Model for India*, Viji Books India, New Delhi, 2013, p. 46.

Based on this idea and drawing on the thinking of the NSAB's SDR 1999, analysts at India's National Security Council (NSC) secretariat developed the Indian National Security Index. The

SDR defined the concept of economic security thus:

> It implies political and economic sovereignty
> and autonomy of decision-making, albeit in an
> increasingly inter-dependent world characterized by
> the 'globalisation' of economic activity. It implies the
> assurance of economic well-being and social justice
> as reflected in particular by generalized access to
> food, clothing, shelter, education and employment. It
> implies the acquisition of skills and knowledge aimed
> at acquiring technical and technological capabilities
> required for sustained and self-reliant economic
> development and assured defence capability.[7]

The SDR summed up the new thinking, thus:

> Clearly, national security encompasses more than
> national defence and internal security. Its foundation
> must rest on the social and economic well-being of
> the people. A socially fractious, economically backward
> and politically divided nation is unlikely to be militarily
> secure. Military security is a necessary, not a sufficient
> condition for national security.[8]

These ideas have since been taken forward by the NSC and the
Ministry of Finance. The NSC commissioned the construction
of what has been termed the National Power Index (NPI).[9] The
NPI was constructed as a weighted average of six quantifiable
variables: economic capability (25 per cent), military
capability (25 per cent), population capability (15 per cent),
technological capability (15 per cent), energy security (10
per cent) and foreign affairs capability (10 per cent). That
the national security establishment had internalized the idea

that economic, technological and human capabilities taken together ought to have a weighting of at least 50 per cent in the NPI, compared to 25 per cent for military capability, stands testimony to the change in thinking on national security in India.

The construction of the NPI spawned several attempts to define what constitutes national power and sovereignty in a globalized world of increasing interdependencies. At the Ministry of Finance, Chief Economic Advisor Dr Kaushik Basu led a research team that constructed what has been called the Index of Government Economic Power (IGEP).[10] The IGEP, composed of four variables, namely, government revenues, foreign currency reserves, export of goods and services, and human capital, is based on the idea that 'the power of a government is its economic power.'[11]

Dr Basu, et al., claim, 'These variables broadly reflect aspects that contribute to a government's economic clout, voice and negotiating leverage by capturing elements like its ability to raise resources, its creditworthiness and credibility in international financial markets, its influence on global economic activity and its potential in terms of human resources.' Arguing that the idea of 'economic power' gained greater importance following the end of the Cold War and the advent of globalization, the authors of IGEP lay particular emphasis on the importance of government intervention and support in post-crisis economies.

The global economic crisis witnessed governments playing a crucial role in stabilizing financial markets and managing to coordinate responses in order to prop up the world economy. In the wake of the crisis, governments continue to play a vital role in terms of economic management and welfare oriented activities. Governments also play a critical role as agents of redistributive equity and development. Therefore, the economic power of governments is a matter of great significance.[12]

Country-wise index numbers were estimated for the years 2000 to 2009 and ranking was done for 100 countries. The US remained at the top, both in 2000 and 2009. China replaced Japan in the second position over the decade, while India moved from the eighth to the fifth rank (Table 14.2). Geopolitical developments in the post-Cold War era have only underscored the point that the competition between nationstates is increasingly—in the economic realm and the idea of national power—linked to economic rather than military power. Military conflict has not been able to resolve any major geopolitical contest, while the global balance of power is increasingly being determined by geo-economic phenomenon.[13]

While trade economists generally emphasize the purely economic and 'rational' reasons for trade liberalization, political economists and strategic policy analysts must also appreciate the 'foreign policy' and 'strategic' dimensions of external liberalization. This relationship manifests itself in two ways: first, increased foreign trade and investment create benign webs of interdependence and mutual benefit with the outside world; second, it increases the cost of a crisis in India to the rest of the world.

Comprehensive National Power

érieureérieure

Comprehensive National Power   147

Table 14.2: IGEP Country Rankings, 2000 and 2009

Country Rank	Country Name 2000	Country Name 2009
1	US	US
2	Japan	China
3	China	Japan
4	Germany	Germany
5	France	India
6	UK	Russia
7	Italy	France
8	India	Brazil
9	Canada	South Africa
10	Brazil	Italy

Source: Basu, Kaushik, et al., 'The Evolving Dynamics of Global Economic Power in the Post-Crisis World: Revelations from a New Index of Government Economic Power,' Department of Economic Affairs, July 2011, pp. 25–34, https://bit.ly/3jCYPpr. Accessed on 9 May 2022.

In the three decades after 1991, India has not only remained an active participant in multilateral economic institutions, but has also woven new webs of interdependence with all major powers, including China, and with a large number of Asian nations. It has also kept defence spending to the minimum, not allowing it to overwhelm the finance ministry's fiscal stabilization agenda. Having protected the national economy from the fallout of economic sanctions imposed in 1998 by the US, Japan and some European countries, when India declared itself a nuclear weapons power, the Vajpayee government legislated fiscal discipline into law by passing the

Fiscal Responsibility and Budget Management (FRBM) Bill, 2000, as an act of Parliament in 2003. The FRBM Act 2003, was an important step in the direction of strengthening the government's fiscal capacity to deal with both internal and external pressures. The Act specified a timetable for reducing and maintaining the fiscal deficit-to-GDP ratio at 3 per cent. It also sought to bring about greater transparency in the government's fiscal management and accountability.[14]

Remaining open to trade flows and proper management of public finance were the two lessons learnt from the 1991 crisis. Over the subsequent two decades, the economy grew at around 7.5 per cent per year, attaining the highest ever rates of close to 9 per cent during 2003–2008, while becoming more globally integrated and ensuring sound macroeconomic management at home. India even managed to withstand the impact of the Asian financial crisis of 1997–1998, which preceded the economic sanctions imposed after the 1998 Pokhran-II nuclear tests. The economy managed to ward off the immediate impact of the transatlantic financial crisis in 2008, and Prime Minister Manmohan Singh was appreciated for his thoughtful leadership at the G20 summit held in Washington D.C. in November 2008, in response to the crisis. However, with time, the global economic crisis that followed the transatlantic financial crisis also hurt India. The slowdown in global trade, the impasse in multilateral trade negotiations and a deterioration in India's fiscal health began to impact growth.

After 2016, when the Modi government undertook the not-so-fruitful demonetization experiment, the Indian economy began to slow down. This slowdown was made worse by the Covid-19 pandemic. As we have seen earlier, the post-Independence growth trajectory of the Indian economy is summed up by three numbers—3.5, 5.5 and 7.5—the annual average growth rates for the periods 1950–1980, 1980–2000 and 2000–2015. Over the five years 2015–2019, the average annual rate of growth has been variously estimated to have been between 5.8 and 6 per cent per annum. This is clearly below the early twenty-first-century average of 7.5 per cent. What is more worrying is that many economists expect the average annual growth rate in the period 2020–2025 to be even lower at between 5 per cent to 6 per cent.[15] This medium-term slowdown will alter the trajectory of India's rise. Therefore, it is necessary that the government prepare a medium-term plan and roadmap for revival of investment, consumption, employment and India's share of world trade for the country to ensure its historic 'tryst with destiny', regaining its status as one of the world's major economies. In the 75th year of Independence, the Modi government has tried to bring the focus back to economic growth and industrial development. It remains to be seen how successful the government will be in taking economic growth back to the trajectory of 8 per cent per year.

Conclusion

Moving Towards Sustainable Development

In 2015, members of the United Nations General Assembly (UNGA) adopted what has come to be called '2030 Agenda for Sustainable Development'. The UN member countries set for themselves and the global community 17 sustainable development goals (SDGs) to be attained by 2030.[1] These are:

1. No poverty
2. Zero hunger
3. Good health and well-being
4. Quality education
5. Gender equality
6. Clean water and sanitation
7. Affordable and clean energy
8. Decent work
9. Industry, innovation and infrastructure
10. Reduced inequality
11. Sustainable cities and communities
12. Responsible consumption and production
13. Climate action

14. Life below water
15. Life on land
16. Peace, justice and strong institutions
17. Partnerships for the goals

While the Covid-19 pandemic and the global geopolitical situation would have made attaining some of these goals by 2030 more difficult, they remain the stated objective of public policy worldwide. If India's development experience over the past 75 years is evaluated against these goals, it is evident that despite all the impressive achievements thus far, India has to travel some distance and fairly rapidly to attain many of them. The accelerated growth process of the period 2000–2015 did bring poverty, the first goal, down sharply. However, the recent growth slowdown along with the impact of the Covid-19 pandemic and the lockdown of the economy has been accompanied by an increase in the population regarded as poor. A revival of growth and the creation of new employment opportunities will remain a priority for any government.

Attaining each of the 17 SDGs, including key objectives, such as universal health care and education, climate action and social justice, will remain important challenges in the near term. Climate change will remain a major challenge for India's further rise. While India has been committed to climate action and has taken several measures to promote the use of renewables and clean energy, and reduce carbon emissions, the policy goal of fostering rapid industrialization, housing for all, mass transportation and better infrastructure, and so on, will make the challenge of reducing the carbon footprint that much more difficult. In the coming years, negotiating this global agenda and making the growth process environmentally and ecologically sustainable will remain a major policy goal.

Many years ago, when India's population size was much smaller, Mahatma Gandhi understood the enormous nature of the challenge that planet earth would face trying to provide enough for all and expressed his warning in these simple words: 'The world has enough for everyone's need, but not for everyone's greed.' This statement has since come to shape global thinking on climate action. The excessive use of fossil fuels, the high consumption and ecologically wasteful and destructive lifestyles of the rich in all nations, and the human abuse of nature in pursuit of excessive and extravagant consumption have all combined to harm the environment and have contributed to climate change. Many in the developing world have rightly asserted that much of this damage has been inflicted on planet earth by developed economies, mostly the countries of North America, Europe and East Asia. In seeking to reduce carbon emissions, the developed countries should not force low- and medium-income countries to forego development opportunities.[2]

The Indian view was clearly articulated as early as 1972 by Prime Minister Indira Gandhi, who took a keen interest in environmental challenges to development and the protection of the environment, when she told the first UN Conference on Environment:

> There are grave misgivings that the discussion on ecology may be designed to distract attention from the problems of war and poverty. We have to prove to the disinherited majority of the world that ecology

and conservation will not work against their interest
but will bring an improvement in their lives.[3]

Over the years, the international community has tried to come
to grips with the problem of global warming and climate
change and identified the reduction of carbon emissions as
a key policy goal. The Indian government chose to adopt
a proactive approach even as it has sought to highlight
the culpability of rich, industrialized nations. In 2008, the
Government of India adopted a National Action Plan on
Climate Change and constituted eight national missions.
These are national missions on solar energy, energy efficiency,
sustainable habitat, sustainable agriculture, water, Himalayan
ecosystem, Green India and strategic knowledge for climate
change.[4]

A report of the Ministry of Earth Sciences presents a
detailed assessment of the impact of climate change on
the Indian subcontinent. In a worst-case scenario, India is
expected to experience a rise in average temperatures in the
range of 4.7 degrees centigrade to 5.5 degrees centigrade, with
the Indo-Gangetic plain and coastal regions facing the worst
impact of climate change.[5] However, India has also echoed
concerns about what has been dubbed 'carbon colonialism'—
the developed countries' attempt to shift carbon dioxide
emitting technologies to developing countries, such as China
and India, and claiming that they do better on emission
reduction than the latter.

While resisting pressures from the developed nations in
dealing with climate change, India has decided not just be
a part of the problem but also an active part of the solution.
The Indian approach to climate change and climate action

has been best summarised in an excellent collection of essays by Navroz Dubash that looks at the science, economics, technology and politics of climate change and presents a comprehensive account of India's approach.[6]

India's principal challenge today is, in many ways, not very different from the challenge it faced at the time of Independence, namely, to eliminate hunger, banish poverty, educate all its citizens and ensure that their healthcare needs are adequately met. India has graduated from the ranks of a 'low-income' economy, according to the old classification of countries adopted by the World Bank, to being classified as a 'low-middle income' economy. On the other hand, China has moved up into the ranks of 'upper-middle income' economies. India will certainly continue to rise, but it requires constant and conscious effort.

For years, development economists have argued that a rising population imposes a huge burden and constrains India's growth. They are partly correct. A less-populated India would have been able to show better results for all its efforts. However, high population can be both a curse and a boon. It is a curse if people are not healthy, educated and productively employed. It is a boon if people are, in fact, healthy, educated and employed. China, too, has a large population, but its investment in human capability has enabled it to develop more rapidly. India has successfully reduced the rate of population growth in most parts of the country. The problem today is less about numbers and more about human capabilities. Increasing investment in education and skills and creating a knowledge-based society and economy is what will take India forward.

Since I have written this book for young Indians, the

millennials who will live through most of the twenty-first century, it is imperative that this generation and successive generations understand the nature of the domestic and global challenges we face and their impact and implications for future growth and welfare. It is now increasingly clear that on many fronts and for several reasons, the past does not offer a perfect roadmap to the future. This book has tried to summarize the Indian development experience over the past 75 years; however, the next 75 will be very different, and we already see the kind of changes we need to make to be able to make the journey forward so that we are able to ensure the well-being and livelihood security of all, and unleash the creativity of every citizen of our democratic republic, irrespective of caste, class, religion or region.

Acknowledgements

When Rupa Publications invited me to write a book that chronicled the rise and fall, the triumph and tribulations of the Indian economy, I accepted gladly. I am grateful to the publisher and editors for giving me this opportunity to look back at the journey of the Indian economy in the 75 years since Independence. In this book, I have drawn on the work of several distinguished economists and so, I am grateful to all of them for their fascinating and comprehensive analysis of economic development in India. I have mentioned in the endnotes several books that deserve to be read by those interested in further, more detailed explorations of this economic journey.

While writing this book I received valuable assistance from Nikita Singla and am truly grateful to her for her time and enthusiastic support. I am grateful to my editors at Rupa for improving the text. I have written this book for young people and for the laypersons who wish to understand the salient features of India's economic rise as it re-emerged from colonial rule, reinvested in development and re-engaged the world.

Notes

CHAPTER 1: FROM DOMINANCE TO 'THE DRAIN'

1   Maddison, Angus, *The World Economy: A Millennial Perspective*, *Development Centre Studies*, OECD Publishing, Paris, 2001.

2   Maddison, Angus, 'The West and the Rest in the World Economy, 1000–2030: Maddisonian and Malthusian Perspectives', *World Economics*, Vol. 9, No. 4, October–December 2008, https://bit.ly/3IKO8LP. Accessed on 15 March 2022. The 'international dollar' used by Maddison is the Geary-Khamis Dollar that is a hypothetical unit of currency that has the same purchasing power parity that the US dollar had in the United States at a given point in time.

3   Pannikar, K.M., *India and the Indian Ocean: An Essay on the Influence of Sea Power on Indian History*, George Allen & Unwin, London, 2nd edn., 1951, p. 23. Other important studies of Indian maritime activity in the Indian Ocean region include: Gupta, Ashin Das, *The World of the Indian Ocean Merchant, 1500–1800*, Oxford University Press, New Delhi, 2001; Fuber, Holden, et al., *Maritime India: Rival Empires of Trade in the Orient, 1600–1800*, Oxford University Press, New Delhi, 2004; Sridharan, R., *A Maritime History of India*, Publications Division, Govt of India, 1982; Chaudhuri, K.N., *Trade and Civilisation in the Indian Ocean: An Economic History from the Rise of Islam to 1750*, Cambridge University Press, UK, 1985.

4   Ibid. 35.

5   Braudel, Fernand, *Civilization and Capitalism, 15th-18th Century: Volume II: The Wheels of Commerce*, translated by Siân Reynold, University of California Press, Oakland, 1992.

6   Braudel, Fernand, *Civilization and Capitalism, 15th-18th Century: Volume III: The Perspective of the World*, translated by Siân Reynold, University of California Press, Oakland, 1992, p. 484.

7   Chanda, Nayan, *Bound Together: How Traders, Preachers, Adventurers and Warriors Shaped Globalisation*, Penguin Viking, New Delhi, 2007, p. 48.

8   Levi, Scott C., *Caravans: Indian Merchants on the Silk Road*, Allen Lane, India, 2015.

9   Subrahmanyam, Sanjay, 'Of Imârat and Tijârat: Asian Merchants and State Power in the Western Indian Ocean, 1400 to 1750', *Comparative Studies in Society and History*, Vol. 37, No. 4, October 1995, pp. 750–780, https://doi.org/10.1017/S0010417500019940. Accessed on 16 May 2022.

10   Maddison, Angus, *The World Economy: A Millennial Perspective, Development Centre Studies*, OECD Publishing, Paris, 2001, p. 115.

11   Dalrymple, William, *The Anarchy: The East India Company, Corporate Violence and the Pillage of an Empire*, Bloomsbury Publishing, New Delhi, 2019.

12   Naoroji, Dadabhai, *Poverty and Un-British Rule in India*, Swan Sonnenschein & Co., London, 1901.

CHAPTER 2: NATIONAL MOVEMENT AND ECONOMIC THINKING

1   Patnaik, Utsa and Prabhat Patnaik, 'Drain of Wealth: Colonialism before the First World War', *Monthly Review*, 1 February 2021, https://bit.ly/3qLmGat. Accessed on 29 March 2022.

2   Ibid.

3   Blyn, George, *Agricultural Trends in India, 1891–1947: Output, Availability, and Productivity*, University of Pennsylvania Press, Philadelphia, 1966.

4   Tagore, Rabindranath, *Nationalism*, Macmillan and Co. Limited, London, 1917, p. 53.

5   Kale, V.G., 'The Present Economic Condition of India', *Towards Development Economics: Indian Contributions 1900–1945*, J. Krishnamurthy (ed.), Oxford University Press, New Delhi, 2009, p. 16.

6   Coyajee, Jehangir C., 'Arguments for Protection', *Towards Development Economics: Indian Contributions 1900–1945*, J. Krishnamurthy (ed.), Oxford University Press, New Delhi, 2009, pp. 63–84.

7   'The Social and Economic Structure' in Bettelheim, Charles, *India Independent*, MacGibbon & Kee Ltd, London, 1968.

8   Chakrabarty, Bidyut, 'Jawaharlal Nehru and Planning, 1938–41: India at the Crossroads', *Modern Asian Studies*, Vol. 26, No. 2, May 1992, p. 282, https://doi.org/10.1017/S0026749X00009781. Accessed on 4 May 2022.

CHAPTER 3: PLANNING FOR FREE INDIA

1   *Proceedings of the National Planning Committee*, National Planning Committee, 1940, https://bit.ly/3Nsihmp. Accessed on 28 March 2022.

2   Ibid. 15.

3   National Planning Committee, *Report of the National Planning Committee 1938*, Indian Institute of Applied Political Research, 1988, https://bit.ly/39nNCaq. Accessed on 16 May 2022.

4   Mariwala, Vibhav, 'Don't Blame Nehru's Socialism for Air India Fate. Read the 1944 Bombay Plan First', *ThePrint*, 26 October 2021, https://bit.ly/3JhWziI. Accessed on 28 March 2022.

5   Thakurdas, Purshottamdas, et al., *A Brief Memorandum Outlining a Plan of Economic Development for India*, Bombay, 1944, https://bit.ly/3soSNOa. Accessed on 4 May 2022. For a copy of the document and a detailed critique, see Baru, Sanjaya and Meghnad Desai (eds.), *The Bombay Plan: Blueprint for Economic Resurgence*, Rupa

Publications, New Delhi, 2018.

6   Ibid.

7   Planning Commission, *1st Five Year Plan*, NITI Aayog, https://bit.
      ly/3wj8jNX; Planning Commission, *2nd Five Year Plan*, NITI Aayog,
      https://bit.ly/3whiUsB. Accessed on 16 May 2022.

8   Banerjee, B.N., G.D. Parikh and V.M. Tarkunde, *People's Plan
      for Economic Development of India*, Post-War Reconstruction
      Committee of the Indian Federation of Labour, 1944, https://bit.
      ly/38t9UaJ. Accessed on 4 May 2022.

9   Kumarappa, J.C., *Gandhian Economic Thought*, Sarva Seva Sangh
      Prakashan, Varanasi, 1951.

10   Ibid. 18.

11   Ibid. 34.

12   Ibid. 52.

CHAPTER 4: STATE AND THE ECONOMY

1   Planning Comission, 1st Five Year Plan, 'Chapter: 1: Planning:
      Economic and Social Aspects', NITI Aayog, https://bit.ly/3wewHAe.
      Accessed on 5 May 2022.

2   Ibid.

3   Ibid.

4   Raj, K.N., 'Indian Planning: Outline of a Critique and an Alternative
      Approach', *Alternate Policies for the Fourth Five Year Plan*, State
      Planning Board, Government of Kerala, Trivandrum, 1969.

5   Planning Commission, *2nd Five Year Plan: Chapter 2: Approach
      to the Second Five Year Plan*, NITI Aayog, https://bit.ly/3N6aWrZ.
      Accessed on 5 May 2022.

6   Ibid.

7   Baru, Sanjaya, 'State and Industrialisation in a Postcolonial
      Capitalist Economy: The Experience of India', *Economic and
      Political Weekly*, Vol. 23, No. 4, 23 January 1988, pp. 143–150,
      https://bit.ly/3wiW5oA. Accessed on 16 May 2022.

8   'Industrial Policy Resolution 1948', in Mohanta, Tapan Kumar,

Industrial Policy of India: A Study of Public Policy, 1999, University of North Bengal, PhD Dissertation, https://bit.ly/3NcICVu. Accessed on 5 May 2022.

9   Government of India, *Industrial Policy Resolutions*, 30 April 1956, https://bit.ly/3wdE89r. Accessed on 5 May 2022.

10 'Social and Economic Aspects of Intermediate Regimes', in Kalecki, Michał, *Selected Essays on the Economic Growth of the Socialist and Mixed Economy*, Cambridge University Press, 1972, pp. 162–169.

11 'Bureaucracy and the Military', in Baru, Sanjaya, *India's Power Elite: Class, Caste and a Cultural Revolution*, Penguin Random House India, New Delhi, 2021.

12 Jana, Jaydev, 'The Poverty Battle', *The Statesman*, 18 February 2021, https://bit.ly/3v5OO4H. Accessed on 8 April 2022.

CHAPTER 5: THE INDIAN EXPERIMENT

1   Thakurdas, Purshottamdas, et al., *A Brief Memorandum Outlining a Plan of Economic Development for India*, Bombay, 1944, https://bit.ly/3soSNOa. Accessed on 4 May 2022.

2   Sheel, Alok, 'Milton Friedman and India', *The Economic Times*, 2 February 2007, https://bit.ly/3JPpgDK. Accessed on 28 March 2022

3   Ibid.

4   Friedman, Milton, 'A Memorandum to the Government of India, 1955', *Foundations of India's Political Economy,* Subroto Roy and William James (eds.), Sage Publications, New Delhi, 1992, p. 164,

5   Ibid. 176.

6   For an exhaustive account of foreign economic interest in Indian development, see Rosen, George, *Western Economists and Eastern Societies: Agents of change in South Asia, 1950-70*, Oxford University Press, New Delhi, 1985.

7   Aiyar, Shankkar, 'India Uses Democratic Superiority Card at WEF Summit to Cover Growth Inability', *India Today*, 13 February 2006, https://bit.ly/3KGNwbC. Accessed on 13 April 2022.

CHAPTER 6: A DECADE OF CRISES

1 Nagaraj, R., 'Growth Rate of India's GDP, 1950-51 to 1987-88: Examination of Alternative Hypotheses', *Economic and Political Weekly*, 30 June 1990, https://bit.ly/3670Zui. Accessed on 13 April 2022.

2 'Private Foreign Investment and Economic Development', in Prasad, S. Benjamin and Anant R. Negandhi, *Managerialism for Economic Development Vol. 11: Studies in Social Life*, Springer, Dordrecht, 1968.

3 'The Economic Consequences of the Kargil Conflict for India and Pakistan', in Baru, Sanjaya, *Strategic Consequences of India's Economic Performance*, Academic Foundation, New Delhi, 2006, pp. 423-424.

4 'A Sketch of Political and Macroeconomic Developments from 1964 to 1991', in Joshi, Vijay and I.M.D. Little, *India: Macroeconomics and Political Economy, 1964-1991*, Oxford University Press, New Delhi, 1994, p. 48.

5 Shah, Paarth, 'Economic Milestone: Devaluation of the Rupee (1966)', *Forbes India*, 11 August 2014, https://bit.ly/3JmYgdW. Accessed on 11 April 2022.

6 For a detailed discussion of the crisis years and the policy response to these multiple crises see, 'A Sketch of Political and Macroeconomic Developments from 1964 to 1991', in Joshi, Vijay and I.M.D. Little, *India: Macroeconomics and Political Economy, 1964-1991*, Oxford University Press, New Delhi, 1994.

CHAPTER 7: ECONOMIC POLICY TURNS LEFT

1 Panagariya, Arvind, *India: The Emerging Giant*, Oxford University Press, New Delhi, 2008, p. 5.

2 Khanna, Sundeep, 'Backstory: The Bank Nationalisation of 1969—Indira Gandhi's Political Masterstroke', CNBC TV 18, 17 August 2021, https://bit.ly/3IZEKnH. Accessed on 4 April 2022.

3   'Plan for Social Control of Banks', *The Hindu*, 14 December 2017, https://bit.ly/36TqVdl. Accessed on 4 April 2022.

4   Quoted in Nayar, Baldev Raj, *India's Mixed Economy*, Popular Prakashan, Bombay, 1989, p. 295. Much of the discussion in this chapter is based on Section C of the book.

5   'History of Insurance in India', Insurance Regulatory and Development of India, 31 July 2020, https://bit.ly/38jFirD. Accessed on 4 April 2022.

6   Jaffrelot, Christophe and Pratinav Anil, *India's First Dictatorship: The Emergency, 1975–77*, Oxford University Press, New York, 2020, p. 294.

7   Quoted in Nayar, Baldev Raj, *India's Mixed Economy*, Popular Prakashan, Bombay, 1989, p. 297.

8   Ibid.

9   Ibid. 320.

10   Economic Survey 1975, 'Chapter 1: The Economy in 1974-1975', Introduction, https://bit.ly/3rmtbRp. Accessed on 13 April 2022.

CHAPTER 8: ECONOMIC POLICY SHIFTS RIGHT

1   Joshi, Vijay and I.M.D. Little, *India: Macroeconomics and Political Economy, 1964-1991*, Oxford University Press, New Delhi, 1994, p. 105.

2   Ibid. 105.

3   Ibid. 113.

4   'Memorial Meeting for I.G. Patel', Reserve Bank of India Bulletin, 13 October 2005, https://bit.ly/3LEieT1. Accessed on 5 April 2022.

5   For a detailed discussion see 'Phase 3 (1981–88): Libralization by Stealth' in Panagariya, Arvind, *India: The Emerging Giant*, Oxford University Press, New Delhi, 2008.

6   Joshi, Vijay and I.M.D. Little, *India: Macroeconomics and Political Economy, 1964-1991*, Oxford University Press, New Delhi, 1994, p. 169.

7   Patel, I. G. 'On Taking India into the Twenty-First Century (New

Economic Policy in India)', *Modern Asian Studies*, Vol. 21, No. 2, April 1987, pp. 209–231, https://doi.org/10.1017/S0026749X00013780. Accessed on 16 May 2022.

8   Joshi, Vijay and I.M.D. Little, *India: Macroeconomics and Political Economy, 1964-1991*, Oxford University Press, New Delhi, 1994, pp. 190–191.

CHAPTER 9: CHANGES IN THE AGRARIAN AND REGIONAL LANDSCAPES

1   Aiyar, S.A., 'Drought Not a Big Calamity in India Anymore', *The Times of India*, 29 July 2012, https://bit.ly/3ud0R5H. Accessed on 6 April 2022.

2   'India at a Glance', *Food and Agriculture Organization of the United Nations*, https://bit.ly/3r8dA81. Accessed on 6 April 2022.

3   Planning Commission, *1st Five Year Plan*, 'Chapter 12: Land Policy', NITI Aayog, https://bit.ly/3yFhutC. Accessed on 16 May 2022.

4   Thakurdas, Purshottamdas, et al., *A Brief Memorandum Outlining a Plan of Economic Development for India*, Bombay, 1944, https://bit.ly/3soSNOa. Accessed on 4 May 2022. For a copy of the document and a detailed critique, see Baru, Sanjaya and Meghnad Desai (eds.), *The Bombay Plan: Blueprint for Economic Resurgence*, Rupa Publications, New Delhi, 2018, p. 307.

5   Rudolph, Lloyd and Susanne Rudolph, *In Pursuit of Lakshmi: The Political Economy of the Indian State*, Chicago University Press, Chicago, 1987, pp. 49–51.

6   Ibid. 50.

7   Ibid. 52.

8   For a more detailed discussion of these issues see 'The Landed and the Feudals' in Baru, Sanjaya, *India's Power Elite: Class, Caste and a Cultural Revolution*, Penguin, New Delhi, 2021.

9   Mitra, Ashok, *Terms of Trade and Class Relations: An Essay in Political Economy*, Taylor and Francis, London, 1977, p. 101.

10   Awasthi, Rahul, 'Break the Agricultural Black Money Shelter and

Tax the Rich Farmer', *The Wire*, 2 May 2017, https://bit.ly/38wSWrI. Accessed on 6 April 2022.

11   Bharadwaj, Krishna, 'Regional Differentiation in India', *Industry and Agriculture in India since Independence*, T.V. Sathyamurthy (ed.), Oxford University Press, Delhi, 1995, p. 209.

12   PTI, 'Focus on Providing Urban Amenities in Rural India: APJ Kalam', 6 February 2012, *The Economic Times*, https://bit.ly/3x4pCTH. Accessed on 6 April 2022.

CHAPTER 10: TOWARDS INDUSTRIALIZATION

1   For a more detailed discussion of industrial policy in the 1950s and after, see Marathe, Sharad S., *Development and Regulation: The Indian Policy Experience of Controls Over Industry*, Sage Publications, New Delhi, 1986.

2   Tendulkar, Suresh and T.N. Srinivasan, *Reintegrating India with the World Economy*, Columbia University Press, New York, 2003.

3   Sharma, Vaishali Basu, 'Why India's MSME Sector Needs More Than a Leg-Up', *The Wire*, 5 July 2020, https://bit.ly/3LSmWwq. Accessed on 12 April 2022.

4   Nayyar, Deepak (ed.), *Industrial Growth and Stagnation: The Debate in India*, Oxford University Press, 1994, p. 11.

5   Sandesara, J.C., *Industrial Policy and Planning - 1947-91*, Sage Publications, New Delhi, 1992, p. 194.

6   For a more detailed discussion of the business–politics nexus see 'Business and the State', in Baru, Sanjaya, *India's Power Elite: Class, Caste and a Cultural Revolution*, Penguin Viking, New Delhi, 2021.

7   This was the assessment of the *Report of the Industrial Licensing Policy Inquiry Committee*, Ministry of Industrial Development, Government of India, Delhi, 1967. *Report of the Industrial Licensing Policy Inquiry Committee*, Ministry of Industrial Development, 1967, https://bit.ly/3yyHJlv. Accessed on 16 May 2022.

8.   Ibid.

9   *Report of the Committee on Prevention of Corruption*, Ministry of

68   *75 Years of Indian Economy*
Home Affairs, Government of India, 1962, https://bit.ly/3lfwvuc.
Accessed on 14 April 2022.

10 To read more see 'Part IV: Transforming India' in Panagariya,
Arvind, *India: The Emerging Giant*, Oxford University Press, New
Delhi, 2008.

CHAPTER 11: THE REGIME CHANGE OF 1991

1   This chapter draws heavily from my book about Former Prime
Minister P.V. Narasimha Rao's politics, economics and geopolitics
reforms. Excerpt(s) from *1991: How P. V. Narasimha Rao Made
History* by Sanjaya Baru, copyright © Sanjaya Baru 2016, reprinted
by permission of Aleph Book Company.

2   Joshi, Vijay and I.M.D. Little, *India: Macroeconomics and Political
Economy, 1964-1991*, Oxford University Press, New Delhi, 1994, pp.
190–191.

3   Patel, I.G., 'New Economic Policies: A Historical Perspective',
Economic and Political Weekly, 4–11 January 1992, p. 43, https://
bit.ly/3a6CzTu. Accessed on 16 May 2022.

4   Baru, Sanjay, *1991: How P.V. Narasimha Rao Made History*, Aleph
Book Company, New Delhi. 2016, p. 42.

5   Ibid. 42.

6   Ibid.

7   R., Nessan, 'The Crisis of Capitalism in India', *World Socialist Web
Site*, 7 June 1991, https://bit.ly/3xpF9gK. Accessed on 11 April 2022.

8   Ministry of Finance, *Economic Survey 1991-92*, Government of
India, New Delhi, p. 6, https://bit.ly/3xTad9a, Accessed on 25 April
2022.

9   Rao, P.V. Narasimha, *Selected Speeches, Volume I, June 1991-92*,
Publications Division, Ministry of Information and Broadcasting,
Government of India, New Delhi, 1993, p. 4.

10 Majumder, Abhijit, 'How Congress Lost PV Narasimha Rao, Its Hero
of Liberalisation, "Look East" and Israel Policies', *Firstpost*, 28 June
2020, https://bit.ly/3vaK5nh. Accessed on 12 April 2022.

11   Srivastava, Vinay K., 'Reliving the Landmark 1991 Economic Reforms,' *BusinessLine*, 26 July 2021, https://bit.ly/3v469zC. Accessed on 12 April 2022.

12   For a firsthand account, read Rangarajan, C., 'Hop, Skip, Jump', *The Indian Express*, 10 November 2015, https://bit.ly/3js8QWi. Accessed on 12 April 2022.

13   Rao, P.V. Narasimha, 'Prime Minister Rao's July 9 Speech Transcript', The 1991 Project, 9 July 1991, https://bit.ly/37Ng19p. Accessed 16 May 2022.

14   Singh, Manmohan, 'Budget 1991-92 Speech of Shri Manmohan Singh Minister of Finance', Ministry of Finance, Government of India, 24 July 1991, https://bit.ly/39SdmvO. Accessed on 16 May 2022.

15   Ibid.

16   Rao, P.V. Narasimha, *Selected Speeches, Volume I, June 1991-92*, Publications Division, Ministry of Information and Broadcasting, Government of India, New Delhi, 1993, pp. 8–9.

CHAPTER 12: MAKING IN INDIA

1   'Manufacturing, Value Added (% of GDP)—India', The World Bank, https://bit.ly/3JDaqPR. Accessed on 13 April 2022.

2   'India Trade to GDP Ratio 1960-2022', macrotrends, https://bit.ly/3M4nUGu. Accessed 9 May 2022.

3   Mehrotra, Santosh, 'New Industrial Policy Needed, Aligned to Trade Policy', *Financial Express*, 20 May 2019, https://bit.ly/3LYnTDB. Accessed on 13 April 2022.

4   *The Manufacturing Plan: Strategies for Accelerating Growth of Manufacturing in India in the 12th Five Year Plan and Beyond*, Planning Commission, New Delhi, Government of India, https://bit.ly/3jwG2fs. Accessed on 13 April 2022.

5   'Manufacturing Would Contribute 25% of GDP by End of 2022', 25 August 2021, *Mint*, https://bit.ly/3xpuwdS. Accessed on 13 April 2022.

6   Babu, M. Suresh, 'Why "Make in India" Has Failed', *The Hindu*, 20
      January 2020, https://bit.ly/3xlF2CX. Accessed on 13 April 2022.

7   Senthilraja, S. and S. Stanislaus, 'Impact of Make in India on Indian
      Economy', *International Journal of Scientific Research and Review*,
      Vol. 8, No. 1, 2019, pp. 442–448, https://bit.ly/3Mj5emB. Accessed
      on 16 May 2022.

8   Jha, Somesh, 'Unemployment Rate at Four-Decade High of 6.1% in
      2017-18: NSSO Survey', *Business Standard*, 6 February 2019, https://
      bit.ly/3va6NMa. Accessed on 13 April 2022.

9   'Gross Fixed Capital Formation (% of GDP) - India', The World Bank,
      https://bit.ly/3w0z5u8. Accessed 9 May 2022.

10   Sitharaman, Nirmala, 'Budget Speech 2022-23', Union Finance
      Ministry, Government of India, February 2022, https://bit.
      ly/3wnJoY4. Accessed on 16 May 2022.

CHAPTER 13: A SERVICES ECONOMY

1   Mukherjee, Arpita, 'The Service Sector in India', *ADB Economics
      Working Paper Series*, Working Paper No. 352, June 2013, Asian
      Development Bank, Manila, p. 5, https://bit.ly/3Ng66IK. Accessed
      on 16 May 2022.

2   Ibid. 9.

3   Hale, Erin, 'Why Communities Are Key to Rebuilding Life after the
      COVID-19 Pandemic', *uchicago news*, 24 August 2021, https://bit.
      ly/3EXUtDr. Accessed on 25 April 2022.

4   Thapar, Karan, 'Full Text: Why Raghuram Rajan Is Promoting a
      Radical Rethinking of India's Political, Economic Strategies', *The Wire*,
      24 February 2022, https://bit.ly/3M7c7Xl. Accessed on 14 April 2022.

CHAPTER 14: COMPREHENSIVE NATIONAL POWER

1   Rao, P.V. Narasimha, *Selected Speeches, Volume I, June 1991–92*,
      Publications Division, Ministry of Information and Broadcasting,

Government of India, New Delhi, 1993, pp. 8–9.

2 For an elaboration of these ideas, see, 'National Security in an Open Economy', in Baru, Sanjaya, *Strategic Consequences of India's Economic Performance,* Academic Foundation, New Delhi, 2006.

3 For more on this see Baru, Sanjaya, 'Security and Sovereignty in an Open Economy: New Thinking after 1991', in Rakesh Mohan (ed.), *India Transformed: Twenty-Five Years of Economic Reforms,* Brookings Institution Press, Washington D.C., 2018, pp. 188–200.

4 Pilsbury, Michael, *China Debates the Future Security Environment,* National Defence University Press, Washington D.C., 2000.

5 Sen, Amartya and Jean Drèze, *India: Economic Development and Social Opportunity,* Clarendon Press, Oxford, 1995.

6 Singh, P.K., Y.K. Gera and S. Dewan, *Comprehensive National Power: A Model for India,* Viji Books India, New Delhi, 2013.

7 Sanjaya Baru, *Strategic Consequences of India's Economic Performance,* Academic Foundation, New Delhi, 2006, pp. 77–78.

8 Ibid. 89.

9 Kumar, Satish, et al., 'National Power Index', *Foundation for National Security Research,* 2012, https://bit.ly/3sOH77F. Accessed on 9 May 2022.

10 Basu, Kaushik et al., 'The Evolving Dynamics of Global Economic Power in the Post-Crisis World: Revelations from a New Index of Government Economic Power', Department of Economic Affairs, July 2011, https://bit.ly/3jCYPpr. Accessed on 9 May 2022.

11 Ibid. 5.

12 Ibid. 5.

13 For an elaboration of this idea, see Baru, Sanjaya, 'Shifts and Shocks: Understanding Geo-economics and Strategy', in *India and the World: Essays in Geo-economics and Foreign Policy,* Sanjaya Baru (ed.), Academic Foundation, New Delhi, 2016.

14 Ministry of Finance, Department of Economic Affairs, Fiscal Responsibility and Budget Management Act, 2003, 26 August 2003, https://bit.ly/3KBE3T3. Accessed on 14 April 2022.

15   Baru, Sanjaya (ed.), *Beyond Covid's Shadow: Mapping India's Economic Resurgence*, Rupa Publications, New Delhi, 2021. Especially essays by C. Rangarajan, Omkar Goswami, Subramaniam Swamy and Sanjaya Baru.

CONCLUSION: MOVING TOWARDS SUSTAINABLE DEVELOPMENT

1   'UN Adopts New Global Goals, Charting Sustainable Development for people and planet by 2030, United Nations', UN News, 25 September 2015, https://bit.ly/3M3xoS2. Accessed on 14 April 2022.

2   For a passionate and informed view on the role of imperialism and colonialism in contributing to environmental destruction, read Amitav Ghosh's scintillating new book, *Nutmeg's Curse: Parables for a Planet in Crisis*, Penguin Books, New Delhi, 2021.

3   Quoted in Ramesh, Jairam, *India Gandhi: A Life in Nature*, Simon Schuster, India, 2017.

4   Prime Minister's Council on Climate Change, Government of India, *National Action Plan on Climate Change*, Ministry of Environment, Forest and Climate Change, https://bit.ly/3xs2Chv. Accessed on 14 April 2022.

5   Mauskar, J.M. and S. Modak, 'The Imperatives of India's Climate Response', *ORF Occasional Paper*, Observer Research Foundation, New Delhi, October 2021, https://bit.ly/3M44scn. Accessed on 14 April 2022.

6   Dubash, Navroz K., (ed.), *India in a Warming World: Integrating Climate Change and Development*, Oxford University Press, New Delhi, 2019.

Index